I have worked with Vicki Merrill for 12 years. Her approach to strategic planning and accountability is purely the best. Traditional planning processes are easy to understand but under-utilized and over complicated by most. As a result most do not plan or hold knowledge workers accountable on a consistent basis. Top performers want clarity of purpose. They want to know what success looks like companywide and individually. Vicki's approach gets this right without over complicating things or creating full-time employment for strategy consultants.

David Frosh
CEO, Whiskey Hill Partners

Vicki Merrill's leadership courses and hands-on coaching of our executive team re-shaped the way we looked at our business. We finally had real accountability that helped move the needle and made the commitment to build a team of "A" players. I found the morale and attitude across the organization changed as a result of the changes we made.

Lindsey Ueberroth
President, Preferred Hotel Group

After 15 years as Chairman and CEO of Constellation Brands, the time had come in 2007 to pass the CEO role to my brother. While this may seem easy, giving up control of the business after a decade and a half while remaining involved as an active Executive Chairman certainly has its challenges. My year with Vicki as my executive and life coach allowed me to face these challenges with great balance, being available to the CEO and his team as needed yet never directly or indirectly influencing outcomes. It was through Vicki that I really developed the courage to let go and let others lead, the wisdom to realize that knowing what I don't know is far more important than that which I do know, and the compassion to really listen with empathy and not have to have the answers. I am a better resource to all the leaders within Constellation and a better leader in the various philanthropic endeavors that I currently lead as a result of Vicki Merrill's leadership lessons and tools.

Richard Sands
Executive Chairman, Constellation Brands

Vicki, hands down, is the best presenter and consultant in the area of maximizing employee performance and energizing cultural change in an organization. I knew Vicki years ago when she was running large health insurance operations, and was impressed at that time with her awesome leadership and management skills. Since then, she's parlayed her personal expertise and that of her clients to be an outstanding presenter, consultant, executive coach, and strategic planning guide.

Mimi Grant
President, Adaptive Business Leaders Organization

10 Simple Secrets
of the
Best Leaders

How To Define Success and Make It Happen!

by Vicki Merrill

A Lightning Source Book
Published by Lightning Source
1246 Heil Quaker Blvd.
La Vergne, TN USA 37086

Copyright 2012 by Vicki Merrill
Book design by Dori Beeler
Cover design by Dori Beeler

For information regarding special discounts for bulk purchases, please contact Lightning Source at: inquiry@lightningsource.com
Phone: (615) 213-5815

ISBN: 978-0-615-61149-5

Every effort has been made to make this book as complete and as accurate as possible. However, there may be mistakes, both typographical and in content. Therefore, this text should be used only as a general guide and not as the ultimate source of leadership information. Furthermore, this manual contains information that is current only up to the printing date.

The purpose of this manual is to educate and entertain. The advice and strategies contained herein may not be suitable for your situation. You should consult with a professional where appropriate. The author and publisher shall have neither liability nor responsibility to any person or entity with respect to any loss or damage caused, or alleged to have been caused, directly or indirectly, by the information contained in this book.

If you do not wish to be bound by the above, you may return this book to the publisher for a full refund.

*To Dave and Ann Ferry, parents who taught me
that happiness is a choice
and that all other choices are limitless.*

Table of Contents

---- ✳ ----

Chapter 5: Secret 4 – Holding People Accountable   51
The secret to doing it without being a jerk

Chapter 6: Secret 5 – Packing Your Team with Talent   68
How to recruit, hire, develop and retain for competitive advantage

Chapter 7: Secret 6 – Creating Communication Magic   82
Your single most important leadership edge

Chapter 8: Secret 7 – Handling Jerks and Conflict   104
The Conflict Management Guidebook

Acknowledgements

As you will learn in this book, I owe much of my success to mistakes – big, nasty, horrible mistakes that helped me learn the fast and hard way how to be a better leader. Luckily, there have been caring, wonderful people along the way who have tried to save me from myself. To these people, too many to mention – but they know who they are – I owe a great debt, as they saved me time, humiliation and the needless suffering of the people who worked for me.

I am grateful for my wonderful clients who had the courage to invite me into their heads, let me wander around inside that amazing space, and learn about both business and life from their talented perspectives.

A huge thanks goes to Dianne Pusch and the wonderful leaders of University of Phoenix who pushed me to finally write this book, although Diane needs no instruction. She is simply a quintessential leader.

I am also very grateful to David Frosh, a dynamic leader, trusted partner and great friend who is the perfect role model for the teachings in this book.

Special gratitude goes Rick Rawson, Pat Donahue and Mimi Grant, inspirational, charismatic and professional leaders all. Thanks isn't enough for Richard Sands, who got inside my head as much as I got inside his, and I know I was the better for the journey. And to Lindsey Ueberroth, who I believe will be known as one of the finest leaders of her generation.

Thanks are due to all who were instrumental in making this book happen: to Malinda Terreri, my talented sister, author and dear friend who knows everything I don't and is willing to take the time to teach me. And to Sandra Rea who painstakingly and skillfully edited a novice's first writing attempt. Several others helped Sandra with this Herculean task and made the book much more readable as a result: Cher Beall, Diane Ferry, David Frosh, Karen McMenomy, Dori Beeler and especially Malinda Terreri who lovingly dissected every page. I owe them all for taking the time to give me honest feedback amid hectic schedules of their own.

To those who took the time and had the patience to offer creative and exciting input about titles, which you will find peppered throughout this book, I am truly grateful: Katy McGuire, Kris Plachy, Debi Robinson and John Thornton.

As you read this book, you'll see that I am clearly in debt to Stephen Covey, whose thoughtful, courageous work informed my early beliefs about successful management and much of what I believe about business today.

Finally, my deepest thanks to my long-suffering and saintly husband, Scott, who is the Guinea pig for all new management ideas, the one who listens patiently to all my exhausting leadership stories and the one who manages through it all to still love me.

1

Why bother?
Is this book just another flavor of the month?

Thousands of CEOs, leaders and managers spend millions trying to improve their leadership skills and avoid easily remedied, career-derailing mistakes, but few of their attempts actually stick.

Why?

Because many of these same leaders read and try to implement "flavor of the month" self-help books that teach rigid approaches for improving results. These techniques are rarely implemented before the next "new" business technique comes along.

You will meet in this book other CEOs and executives who have taken a different path to avoiding these mistakes and solving many of the same challenges you are probably facing. You will discover the nuts-and-bolts DSAMIH tools they implemented to successfully tackle difficult everyday business situations while taking their organizations a quantum leap forward. By the time you finish this book, you'll see how easy it is to build the qualities that will make you an even more successful and inspirational leader.

I have been fortunate to work with more than 250 companies and 2,500 senior executives over a 30-year period and have learned much from them about what is truly effective in leading people to success. My goal with this book is to share that knowledge with you in a format that is simple, fun and easy to implement.

This book packages a menu of proven leadership tools that can be tailored to the reader's specific needs so that *this time* improvements stick. It includes insights gathered from all these senior executives about their biggest fears and vulnerabilities and how they overcame them with confidence. It offers simple actions steps for avoiding the major derailers of successful leadership, actual case studies that demonstrate the use of these tools and easily referenced "how to's" for solving the most frequent problems facing business leaders today.

10 Simple Secrets of the Best Leaders outlines very clearly well-established techniques that will help you handle the following with ease:

1. How to define success and cascade goals throughout your organization to ensure *achievement* of your success
2. How to create a killer plan for both your business and your life
3. How to pack your team with talent and avoid the top five recruiting and top 10 employee retention mistakes made by most companies
4. How to easily hold people accountable, even if you're a "nice guy" who avoids confrontation
5. How to enhance the essential leadership skill of effective communication
6. How to handle jerks and conflict with confidence
7. How to manage time so that it doesn't manage you
8. How to delegate effectively without worrying about the outcome
9. How to get people to follow you anywhere
10. How to implement what you've learned in this book so that it *sticks*

Many business books offer theory and generalities. *10 Simple Secrets* offers pragmatic "to do" checklists that can be implemented immediately, specific to each type of management issue, along with easy-to-remember bumper sticker summaries to help you recall the lessons most important to you. And if you don't remember... no worries! Simply use the book as a reference tool when an issue arises to quickly find the checklist you need for that specific situation.

I wish I had had these very tangible tools in my own leadership tool kit when I was running my own companies... tools that I could have deployed during the inevitable challenges that face every business leader. I invite you acquire them here the easy way rather than through 30 years of hard experience.

I would suggest using the following guidelines as you read this book:

- *Keep an open mind.* A few of the ideas outlined may sound a little foreign. Wait a day after reading a chapter to pass judgment.
- *Keep it simple.* Not all of the tools in this book apply to you nor will all of them work for you. Adopt the ones that will. Choose two or three that you know will make a difference and try those first.
- *Never assume that what is outlined here is the only way.* There are lots of management techniques that work. Those I include in this book are those that I have seen work repeatedly across all industries, all company sizes and with all types of executives.
- *Make it yours; write notes in this book and highlight.* You can read through each chapter in order, read the chapters independently if you have interest in a specific topic OR use each chapter as a reference when you have an inquiry on that particular topic. I suggest that as you read you *highlight* the concepts that most resonate for you – it will make the powerful assignment at the end of the book that helps you implement your lessons learned an absolute breeze.
- *Have fun!* Life is short; enjoy the process. Learn something new, but don't make it a chore.

This is my challenge to you: find only two or three ideas in this book that will take you and your team to the next level of performance. Then use them to your advantage to *Define Success And Make It Happen*!

2

Secret 1 – What's a DSAMIH?

How to create real alignment and accountability with YOUR team

I believe in bumper stickers. One's ability to reduce to a short, compelling phrase what one truly means is the substance of really memorable communication. You will find persuasive bumper stickers in compelling presidential campaigns, forceful marketing approaches and award-winning commercials on television. You will also find them peppered throughout this book and at the end of each chapter. DSAMIH is just such a bumper sticker.

Having worked with so many successful senior executives and companies of all sizes and industries, I was eager to capture the essence of all I had learned from them in my company's name. It was a daunting task to reduce to a bumper sticker the *one* most important thing I had learned through my work with them in the areas of strategic planning, accountability systems, leadership training and executive coaching.

But it all comes down to this one simple secret of leadership, which I will share with you now: **If you can clearly and compellingly define success, and if everyone in the room agrees with that definition, you can make it happen every time!** Thus the DSAMIH bumper sticker was born – the acronym for:

Define Success And Make It Happen

DSAMIH (pronounced da sahm' ee) – Some say it sounds like a terrorist cult,

Japanese origami or a type of bottled water, none of which my marketing buddies tell me is an appropriate image for a successful business consulting firm, but it is mine. It defines what I do as well as the impact I try to have on each client with whom I work.

I am eager to share with you just how the DSAMIH process has worked for real organizations to consistently improve results, and how the process can work for you and your business, too.

So let's dive into the secret of DSAMIH. In this chapter, you will learn powerful tools for *Defining Success* in your organization, and then how to master the essential *Make It Happen (MIH)* part.

Defining Success

What Do Triangles Have To Do With It?

Defining Success requires that you understand some very important "triangles" so you can harness the energies of everyone in your organization to focus on that which is most important to your success. This may sound a little tricky at first, but it's easier than you might think, and "the process" does much of the work *for* you. What follows is a typical organization chart to help you visualize these triangles.

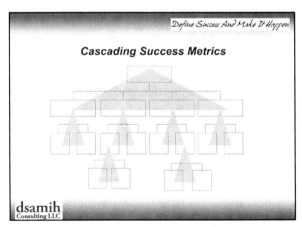

Each triangle represents a manager and his or her direct reports at multiple levels in an organization, with the top triangle being the CEO and his or her team.

It is the responsibility of the CEO and his or her direct reports in the *top triangle* to visualize the future of the organization and to decide what success looks like three to five years from now. This becomes the company's vision.

An organization's vision should outline how big the organization will be in terms of size, revenue, profit and geography. It should identify where the ideal growth will come from in terms of service, product, client type and distribution. Companies need to determine specifically where they want their growth to come from so they can plan proactive strategies for achieving that which is clearly defined as most beneficial to the organization.

You'll learn specific steps for *how* to create a vision quickly and effectively in Chapter 3 on planning as well as what to do if the triangle above *you* hasn't created a plan yet! But wait… why don't we just talk about this now? Because it is important that you understand the big picture process of DSAMIH before we dive into the mechanics of *how* to do it. Bear with me as we look at the next step in *Defining Success*, which involves metrics...

Why Do We Need Success Metrics?

It is also this top triangle's responsibility to determine the top five *success metrics* for monitoring progress toward the vision, and they must be in order of priority. Metrics are important because you can know without measuring that you are doing better in terms of revenue, profitability or customer satisfaction. However, you can only truly know if you are succeeding if you have a measurable target. Let me be even clearer:

> **Success metrics must be specific individual numbers and not spreadsheets, flowery words or great intentions!**

Why only five metrics? You must have a clear, concise and objective way to *know* if you are achieving your plan. Think of the number of plans that never happen because there is no foolproof execution process. These five prioritized measures are the ones most critical to the effective achievement of your vision, and they become part of your fool-proof tool-kit for making it happen.

Why, you may ask, if there are only five measures do they have to be in priority order? As you think about what *your* top five should be, I guarantee there will be some competing pressures on your list. Can you perform well with revenue but not with profit? Can you do great with customer satisfaction but poorly with productivity? Which of these is most important to the success of *your* organization this year? If you and the team in the top triangle don't decide then who will? Right… all the people below you on the organization chart! What are the chances that they will all choose the same priorities as you would? The odds are pretty slim.

Does all this sound daunting? Again, you will find in Chapter 3 on planning a step-by-step outline for determining quickly these important success metrics with *your* team, but let's first finish the *Defining Success* process...

How to Cascade the Metrics in *Your* Organization

Once the top triangle has done this important work as a team and the top five prioritized success metrics for the *organization* are clear we are ready to *Define Success* for each team member in that top triangle.

It is the responsibility of each direct report in that triangle to determine what *his or her* best contributions to the success of the plan will be and how *their* success will be measured. If, as Pareto's 80/20 rule suggests, we are to focus on the 20% of all things which yield the 80% result, each person on that team must limit their priorities to no more than five top goals, and they must be in priority order. Again, not as difficult as you might think.

It is also important that the success metrics of the top triangle direct reports be negotiated *as a team* rather than one-on-one with the leader. These individuals are dependent on one another for success, and they must agree on what each team member's contributions and priorities should be. When conducted effectively, each direct report in that top triangle should know the organization's overall plan or vision and the top five success metrics, in priority order, for monitoring the progress of their *own* contributions to making it happen.

Now to the *next* layer down from the top triangle as we continue to *Define Success* for the organization. Once each top triangle direct report knows his/ her top five success metrics, it is that individual's responsibility to meet with *his or her* triangle of direct reports on the organization chart to cascade the goals down through the organization. All of these top "lieutenants" should show *their* individual team or triangle the organization's vision along with its five prioritized success metrics. Each should then share with their triangle *their own* top five prioritized goals negotiated with their peers in the top triangle. Each then asks of their direct reports the two magic accountability questions:

Now that you know the company's vision, the scorecard for the whole organization and how *I* will be measured...

1. What are *your* most important contributions and
2. How can we measure *your* success?"

Cory, the CEO of a fast-growing pharmaceutical supply company, had struggled for years to get all of his employees focused on the right things. He believed that his role was to be constantly vigilant about all they were doing to ensure that critical issues wouldn't slip through the cracks and that their clients were well served. He spent nights and weekends checking on his staff, attempting to catch them doing the wrong things he just knew were happening. His people felt mistrusted and micromanaged.

After completing the DSAMIH business planning process and determining the company's top five success metrics, Cory was relieved and energized to find that all he had to do to get everyone in the organization in alignment with his goals was to share this planning output and ask the magic accountability questions. He was amazed to find how passionate his direct team was in establishing their own ambitious goals and then negotiating measurable contributions with *their* direct reports.

"Wow," he said. "I never would have believed that they would take the ball and run with it like this. They are actually being tougher on themselves than I would have been, and I'm pretty demanding. Don't get me wrong. I think it's great, but why do you think they are responding like this?"

Cory was feeling a little guilty that he had been unable to harness this kind of passion from his team in the past. He had failed to see that his people weren't the enemy to be checked on and chastised, but rather that they were there because they wanted to contribute and make a difference. Further, the employees embraced the DSAMIH process because they saw that this kind of goal-setting and accountability would reduce Cory's need for micromanagement and give them the empowerment they needed to show him how well they really could do their jobs.

Asking Rather Than Telling While *Defining Success*

Why should the leader of each respective triangle ask rather than *tell* people their goals or success metrics? We all know that it is much easier and faster to *tell*, but what is lost in this scenario is both buy-in and perspective. The people actually performing the jobs may just have an important point of view about how best to measure their contributions. They must also own their goals. Have you ever been handed an unrealistic goal? How much commitment and energy did you apply to a goal that you felt unachievable? We want to capture both hearts and minds in this process, so people can contribute their best efforts. You want them on board and you need their points of view.

Finally, one of the most important reasons for *asking* for input is so that peers have a chance to negotiate as a team what they need from each other in order to be successful. This is how to ensure alignment among your people. Here is a example of how that works with two peers: Sally's number-one goal is dependent on Mark's support and they have been in a constant tug of war about the lack of that support over the last two years. In the goal-setting exercise, Mark has listed Sally's top goal as priority number 57 on his list. It is now obvious that these two key contributors on the team are not in alignment. Leaders are better served by negotiating alignment in a room with their teams during a strategy session rather than over the course of a year with real time, money, staff and resources at risk.

How to Avoid Sandbaggers

A few years ago, Steve, a building industry CEO I was working with, blanched when I suggested that he ask rather than tell people their success metrics. He was worried that his team would establish easy goal targets and that the full potential of the organization would not be realized. His fear? He would fail to meet his *own* numbers.

If you are concerned that some of your team will set sandbag goals (ones that are too easy that will simply make them look good with little effort) you can do what Steve did. He learned that having the team negotiate their goals as a group added peer pressure to the equation, causing the sandbaggers to be more accountable.

Steve was delighted to find that the rest of the team actually cared about each of the other team members' goals and exerted pressure on the sandbaggers. He didn't have to intervene or tell the sandbagger to increase his goals, because the team did it for him. Team members want their peers to each carry their own loads so that they don't have to pick up the extra burden. For you "nice guys and gals" out there who have difficulty negotiating challenging but realistic goals with your sandbaggers, you can use this team negotiation process to be the "bad guy" *for* you.

How Far Should You Go?

How far down the organization should you go in *Defining Success* and cascading success metrics? As far down as you want to be effective. Everyone in the organization should know how what they do contributes to the overall success of the team and that each person's actions matter.

Unfortunately, as a consultant, I have opportunities to speak with disgruntled and disenfranchised employees more often than any leader would want to know about. Many managers believe that their employees' frustration comes from their belief that they don't make enough money. What workers often confess to me – a consultant who has no influence on their future or income – is that they are working hard, sometimes nights and weekends, but they don't think that the leaders above them even *know* what they do let alone what their work contributions are. Here's what I've learned is the key:

All employees want to be part of something that is bigger than they are, that they are proud of, to which they make a tangible contribution.

Everyone wants to make a difference. If you fail to connect each person in your organization to your overall success, you fail to capture the full energy and potential of your team.

Cascading success metrics throughout your organization that are in alignment with your vision is what *Defining Success* is all about. And it is a powerful first step toward quantum leaps forward in achieving the results you are striving for.

Hundreds of my clients have successfully used this process to define and communicate success in their organizations and to negotiate success metric contributions with each of their employees so that *all* are in alignment with their vision and with each other. You will learn exactly *how* they did that in the next chapter.

But now that we've reviewed the *Define Success* part of DSAMIH, let's look at the oh-so-important *And Make It Happen* part, which is how you ensure the effective execution of your vision and success metrics once you have cascaded them throughout your organization.

Making It Happen (MIH):

Many companies do a good job of establishing goals. In fact, I remember asking a young woman last year if her organization had goals. She replied that it did and that they went through the process every year around "budget season." I then asked her what *her* goals were. She looked rather annoyed, reached behind her, pulled out a big, dusty notebook and started rifling through it. She was searching for her goals. What were the chances she had actually *achieved* her goals that year? The lesson here is that there is only way to ensure that goals are actually achieved:

You must inspect what you expect.

How to Inspect What You Expect

Organizations have demonstrated a wide range of techniques for doing just that. Some establish the goals as outlined above and then put them in those big, dusty notebooks. They pull them out around performance review time each year... and sometimes not even then.

Some take it a step further and actually publish monthly results against the negotiated goals. With that action, everyone knows where he/she stands in the organization, but if they stop there, they are simply changing their goals to fit their results. They aren't changing any behaviors that will help them recover from those unfavorable results.

Other companies take it one step further. For any goal not met, the goal owner is required to outline his/her issues, obstacles, challenges, whines and excuses – all the things that got in the way of making the goal. An improvement. Now, for any goal not met, they are drilling down to find out what went wrong. But if they stop there, they create a culture where a good excuse is as good as a good result.

Let me share with you how that works. An employee goes to an accountability meeting, armed with a long, fascinating story to explain why he or she didn't meet a goal. The team actually feels sorry for the person, nods their heads in sympathy, and then moves on to the next team member's report. Not real accountability yet, is it?

Are all these issues, obstacles and challenges the person's fault? No. Things happen outside our control. Markets and competitors change. The economy tanks. Stuff happens. Life happens. Other people's actions happen. No one has 100% control. What is under our control is what we decide to *do* about these things.

So in order to be truly accountable, the best leaders take accountability one step further still. They negotiate clear success metrics for each person in the organization, publish the results against those metrics monthly, diagnose the obstacles getting in the way and then *determine corrective actions* in monthly *Make It Happen* meetings.

How to Decide Corrective Actions

For any success metric not met, the goal owner must prepare his or her best diagnosis of the obstacle getting in the way before coming to his or her triangle's monthly *MIH (Make It Happen)* meeting. Each gets one minute during this accountability meeting to explain the diagnosis and reduce the problem to a bumper-sticker question for the team.

The individual must then ask each member of the triangle, including the manager, to offer suggestions for overcoming that obstacle. Sometimes the obstacle is someone else on the team who has failed to follow through with a commitment. If this is the case, it will surface and be resolved quickly. To make this process even clearer, let's just say that the goal owner who didn't hit the success metric is *you*.

You have explained to your team what got in your way and have reduced your issue to a compelling open-ended question. Each of the team members in your triangle, including your manager, will offer several ideas for solving the problem as you move quickly around the group to drill for suggestions. You will often receive as many as 10 to 20 different ideas within minutes.

It is your job in this process to be quiet, receive great (as well as lame) ideas and write them *all* down. You are allowed no *Yabuts*. ("Yabut I've already tried that... Yabut that won't work!") The more you refute the ideas offered, the fewer great suggestions you will receive.

After you have received the best thinking your team has to offer, who should decide the one or two corrective actions that will be taken? *You*, the goal owner, must decide. It would be a mistake to have the manager or the team decide *for* you, because that would take accountability away from you. When the manager decides the corrective action for you, you can simply follow exactly what the manager says to do, and report that you've done exactly as told. Unfortunately you can also add, "By the way, it didn't work!"

Keep accountability with the goal owner. Remember that he or she owns the success metric and must come back in 30 days to present results to the team again during the next monthly *MIH* meeting. If the chosen action fails to deliver a positive result, the goal owner must choose a new action. One of the main benefits of this approach is that no one on the team gets too far off track and all own their metrics. Big, ugly problems in the organization surface quickly and are addressed positively using the best thinking of the team rather than being covered up by goal owners who often fear retribution for talking about problems.

So the goal owner must choose the top two or three actions that he/she believes will best move the needle forward. These commitments are written down, along with who is accountable and a due date for each action.

An action without a due date is a wish.

The triangle's collective action steps, accountable parties and due dates are then published to the team. You will find an easy, step-by-step outline of *how* to run the *Make It Happen (MIH)* meeting in Chapter 5 on holding people accountable.

But in the meantime, ask yourself how far the *Define Success And Make It Happen* process occurs in your organization:

- Do you negotiate the top five goals or success metrics that are in alignment with yours with each of your team members?
- Do you inspect what you expect? Is each team member responsible for publishing results monthly, in writing, to his/her triangle?
- Is each team member responsible for being prepared with a thorough diagnosis for any goal not met?
- Do you use the best thinking of the team to arrive at meaningful corrective actions?
- Does the goal owner decide the corrective action and when specifically it will be completed?
- Are these commitments shared in writing with the team so that all members are aware of and can reference those commitments?

The *DSAMIH* process works for every type of business model. For more than a decade, I have collaborated with universities, hospitals, hotels, real estate companies, financial institutions, manufacturers, builders and other businesses to employ this process for taking their success to the next level. These are the results they consistently see:

- Meetings become less about what people choose to discuss and more about those drivers that are essential to individual and overall business success.
- Leaders of these organizations spend less time chasing people to determine how things are going and more time being chased by goal owners who want to report meaningful results.
- Accountability becomes less about getting employees in trouble for failing and more about rallying talent around an obstacle to get it solved.
- Alignment becomes less about who screams loudest or who is most powerful and more about what is required by each individual so that the entire team can win.
- Team communication improves as all focus on what each team member must do to achieve the agreed-upon goals.

By following the *DSAMIH* process outlined here and in Chapter 3 on business planning and in Chapter 5 on holding people accountable, you can do this for your teams and reap the rewards of clear vision, goal alignment and an execution process that actually works to improve your results!

Summary and Action Steps:

Use the *DSAMIH* process to:

1. *Define success* in a clear vision
   - Communicate that vision clearly to your direct reports (your triangle) and to those beneath them
   - Ask them to determine *their* success metrics and *negotiate* rather than tell people their success metrics
   - Keep them to a few prioritized metrics that align with the company vision
   - Cascade the goals: Have each layer of the organization negotiate success metrics with *their* teams in alignment with this vision and the higher-level organizational metrics

2. *And Make It Happen* by inspecting what you expect. Ensure that all team members:
   - Publish results monthly to their respective triangles or teams
   - Think through the real issues that are preventing achievement of their metrics
   - Use the best thinking of their triangle to determine corrective actions
   - Commit to their chosen actions and to a due date!

DSAMIH **- The Bumper Sticker - Cascade goals throughout your organization and inspect what you expect!**

3

Secret 2 – Powerful Business Plans in Just Two Days!
How YOU can be the architect of your business

We talked in the *DSAMIH* chapter about the importance of creating vision, and I promised you in this chapter a simple process for doing that. Before describing how to do it, I should level with you that based on my work with large and small organizations over the years I have found that about 80% of U.S. companies simply don't plan their futures.

Why?

They have a lot of excuses. They will tell you that they don't have time, they don't know how, they think it's too bureaucratic or that it is a useless exercise that consumes too much time and makes no tangible difference. Sound familiar?

I have worked with leaders of start-up companies experiencing 500% growth who felt they had no time to react to the crisis of the day much less develop a business plan. I have also worked with established, billion-dollar companies whose leaders said, "Hey, we're doing pretty well - why fix what isn't broken?"

Both types learned that they were able to define their desired business success with thoughtful, well-crafted business plans to make it happen, all in just two days. Because of the simple process we worked through together they were able to use the best thinking of their teams to create quick and effective strategic plans that actually happened. Just listen to what some of them have said about the process:

- "I wouldn't have believed it could happen so quickly and be so much fun."
- "I actually dreaded this meeting and it turned out to not only define our future, but it energized our team."
- "I was amazed by how everyone participated. I learned a ton about my own company."
- "We got more done in these two days than we have in years of senior executive meetings."

At DSAMIH, we believe that the Jack Nicklaus approach to playing a new golf course is a good method for developing a powerful plan. Do you know how this world-class golfer approaches a new course that he has never played and hasn't designed? (Which really reduces the number of golf courses!) He walks it backwards. He begins at the 18th hole and walks it from green to tee. Why? Because he wants to play at every vantage point on the course with the end in mind.

We use a similar approach with DSAMIH business planning. It is essential to know clearly where you are and where you want to be in order to reverse engineer a direct path to get there without getting sidetracked.

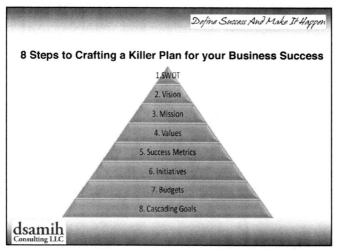

This is the process you will learn in this chapter, where I outline eight easy steps as visualized in yet another triangle above, for building an effective and strategic business plan in only two days, allowing *you* to be the architect of your own business success.

So… ready to get started?

Eight Steps to Crafting a Killer Plan for your Business

Step 1: Situation or SWOT Analysis – Know your starting points. These are your Strengths, Weaknesses, Opportunities and Threats (SWOT), a typical starting approach to business planning. What is not so typical but critical is not only to understand the issues that fall into each of these categories but also to reduce them to your top three points in each category. Why? Remember the 80/20 rule? It is important to simplify and keep your focus on the 20% that achieves the 80% result. Too many business plans get bogged down with long lists of issues that must be resolved. Thoroughness here can result in paralysis. We need to focus on the most important issues in each category.

As you are working through your lists, consider Strengths and Weaknesses to be internal issues. These are things you do to yourself that either help or hurt your competitiveness and are, therefore, things over which you should have a great deal of control. Examples include your product/service, customer/market, operations/efficiency, human resources, facilities, financials and management.

Consider Opportunities and Threats to be external issues. These are things outside your organization that could help or hurt you and over which you have less control, but which you can often influence. Examples include competitive, social, technological, economic, environmental and political influences.

Brainstorm with your team about your Strengths, Weaknesses, Opportunities and Threats. List them all honestly. Actually, when you establish a safe environment, listing the issues in each category comes very easily to most clients. They have animated discussions about each one. They show great pride in their Strengths and lament some of the Weaknesses that have been on the list for years. As I warn them, listing all the possibilities in each category isn't the tough part.

The difficult job is to narrow down your list to the most important three points in each category. These are the ones for which you will develop specific actions in your business plan. This narrowing takes discipline! Don't combine several items on your list just so you can pretend that you've narrowed to three. Have the wisdom to actually choose the three most important Strengths and Weaknesses impacting your company's competitive advantage. Choose the three most important Opportunities and Threats affecting your company's future. Now that you've assessed your current situation, we aren't going to do anything about it yet without looking first into your the future (playing with the end in mind).

Step 2: Your Vision – What is it that you want to get out of your markets in terms of size, revenue and profit? Where do you want that growth to come from in terms of product, service, customer type and geography? Not all clients are equal; in fact, some are unprofitable. Some products and services are lucrative; some are not. Opportunities that arrive on our doorsteps aren't necessarily the ones that are in our best interest. Which are the ones we want to go *after*? You must determine specifically where you want your growth to occur so you can plan proactive strategies for achieving that which is most beneficial to the organization.

And as you visualize your business future (your vision) be positive and specific. Don't talk about what you *don't* want. Instead talk about what you do want. Rather than saying, "We don't want to be unprofitable," say instead, "We want to make $250,000 in EBITDA (earnings before interest, tax, depreciation and amortization)." Don't say we don't want to lose our biggest account, but rather that we want 98% client retention, $1 million in organic growth and $250,000 in new growth this year.

Work as a team to decide what "perfect" looks like three to five years in the future. It may be helpful to you to try an exercise that I use with clients in our vision sessions...

Imagine that you are at a holiday party in five years. Your organization has hit it on all cylinders. How big is it? How profitable? Where did the growth come from? What was important to your success? Visualize what perfect looks like as if it has already happened. Create a list of the top five things you will see when "perfect" is realized – be sure to make them measurable.

As Jack Nicklaus shows us, if you know where you are now (your SWOT) and you know where you're going (your vision), you can reverse engineer to determine what must be done by year to achieve that vision.

Quantum Lenses, a small precision lens company in Texas generating $8 million in revenue went through this very SWOT and vision exercise and in doing so made an important discovery. They had two major product lines: standard-sized, lower-priced lenses that sold in high volume and which represented 50% of their revenue and 25% of their expenses. The other product line involved higher-priced, customized lenses, which sold in low volume and which represented 50% of their revenue and 75% of their expenses!

They loved this second, customized lens market and I had to question why? It seemed to be eating up all their margins. It turns out that the lower-priced, standard lenses required no real expertise or scientific creativity. Once the manufacturing operation was in place, these lenses could be cranked out in high volume and with great reliability. Boring.

The customized lenses were used by film production companies to create high-tech special effects in big-budget movies. Interesting, exciting, challenging and costly to deliver.

Quantum Lenses had an important decision to make when it realized that by eliminating half of its revenue stream (represented by their beloved custom lenses) along with the expenses that went with it they could literally increase profitability by 50%!

They had to decide what business they were actually in and what their real competitive advantage was if they were to achieve their three-year vision, which was to achieve overall revenues of $20 million with 20% EBITDA. They needed to decide their mission...

Step 3: Your Mission – This is a simple, compelling sentence that states your business purpose: why you are here, who you serve and how you want to be remembered by your clients and your employees. It should also reflect your UCA (Unique Competitive Advantage) and become a decision tool for any company at a crossroads, like Quantum Lenses was, on how to best serve its clients and grow its business.

That's a lot to fit in to one, concise bumper sticker, but if you are successful, this will be a statement of purpose of which you can be proud, and which will provide direction to your entire organization!

UCA – *Something you'll need to know in order to have an effective mission:*

What is "your Unique Competitive Advantage" or UCA and how do you incorporate that into your mission? This is an important concept presented by Treacy and Wiersema in their breakthrough book *The Discipline of Market Leaders* in which they suggest that all companies across all industries really have only three basic ways to compete: price, innovation or customer service. No real news there. However, they named these three categories respectively: Operational Excellence, Product/Service Innovation and Customer Intimacy and laid out an explanation for each as follows:

Operational Excellence – *In order to compete on price, you must be known for:*

- Reliability, consistency, standardization, efficiency and high value.
- Low margin requires high volume, quality transactions – you must be an efficient, well-oiled machine.
- What companies compete this way? Wal-Mart, Southwest, FedEx, McDonald's and *the standard lens division of Quantum Lenses.*

Product or Service Innovation

- Known for creativity, flexibility, innovation, the latest technology and solutions.
- Innovation requires out-of-the-box thinking, risk-taking and a willingness to make your own products and services obsolete in order to have the latest thing available on the market. You become a think tank that creates innovations so ahead of market demand that your customers don't even know they want or need this product or service, and for this early-adaptor market you can charge a premium.
- What companies compete this way? Apple, Microsoft, Nike and 3M.

Customer Intimacy

- Known for superior service, customization, hand holding and going the extra mile.
- This kind of breathtaking service requires that you think inside the heads of your specialized customers to create ways to meet their every service

need, and for this high-end market you can charge a hefty premium. In fact, you must do so to cover your one-off expenses!
- What companies compete this way? Nordstrom, Four Seasons, Lexus and the customized lens division of Quantum Lenses.

The new wisdom that Treacy and Wiersema brought to this standard marketing equation was that you must be competitive at all three of the basic ways to compete, but you must be *known* only for one. This one becomes your Unique Competitive Advantage. Why only one?

Let's take a look at what we reward employees for in each of the three scenarios and how confusing these incentives get if a company tries to compete all three ways equally:

Operational efficiency – We reward employees to follow procedure, minimize error and to create efficient, streamlined transactions. Decisions must be centralized. Why? We don't want McDonald's employees to create their own unique recipes. We want them to follow standardized routines and processes *as Quantum Lenses did with their well-oiled standard lens manufacturing operation.*

Product or Service Innovation – We reward employees to think out of the box, make wild mistakes and to dream. We want them to create products and solutions that we imagine our clients will need.

Customer Intimacy – We reward employees to create long-term customer relationships, understanding that the customer is always right and that we live to serve the customers' needs as they perceive them, *as Quantum Lenses wanted to do with their custom lens division, designed to serve the specific high-tech needs of film production companies.*

Look at these competing pressures. How do you incentivize employees to follow the rules and "color *inside* the lines" when it comes to meeting customer needs AND think out of the box to create what customers don't even *know* they need AND do whatever customers *say* they need and do it ASAP? No employee can achieve this kind of conflicting direction. In fact, if you ask them to do all three equally, as many companies do, you will make them schizophrenic! (Okay, I'm being a little dramatic here, but you get my meaning.) Have you noticed a little "schizophrenia" among your employees?

Quantum Lenses did. They realized while in the process of creating their mission that their manufacturing operation had been designed for high-volume, standard lenses. When they enthusiastically brought one-off custom requests to the manufacturing team, what they got in return were defects, delays, re-work and client grievances, all of which were costly on many levels.

Quantum Lenses was at a crossroads. Would they be Operationally Excellent and stick with their standard lens success or would they be Customer Intimate and design not only their manufacturing operation but also their sales, marketing, customer service and all customer touch points around high-service custom work?

They decided not to decide. You'll learn more about that in a minute.

First, let's take a look at UCA from another perspective. Now that we've reviewed how *employees* look at Unique Competitive Advantage, let's take a look at how customers view the issue. Except for Quantum Lenses, the successful companies mentioned above have managed our *customer* expectations. If I were the last to arrive at the Southwest gate and asked for a cushy, first-class seat, the gate agents wouldn't apologize for being unable to accommodate me. They would simply remind me that with their airline, I would get a great fare and the best on-time arrival rate in the industry. Further, they would tell me that if I really needed that first-class seat I'd have to go to another carrier.

I know better than to go to McDonald's and ask for a sushi platter. If I were to do such a thing, the manager in charge would not want his team to stop the assembly line and try to build one for me. And they can't exactly give me an uncooked fish sandwich! McDonald's knows that Operational Excellence is their competitive advantage, and they make no apology for not operating in the other two arenas.

On the other hand, I could go to Four Seasons and even if a sushi platter weren't on their menu they would find a way to make it for me at some exorbitant cost. Why? They know they are operating in the Customer Intimacy arena and that they must not only deliver what I want, but charge a premium for their one-off efforts.

None of the companies listed above struggle with attempts to change their business model if they happen to find customers who want something other than their chosen competitive advantage. In fact, this is the essence of *The Discipline of Market Leaders*... having the *discipline* to stick with your UCA even when some clients try to pull you in a different direction.

Unfortunately, Quantum Lenses didn't have that discipline. They had clients who wanted both Operational Excellence and Customer Intimacy, and although their one assembly line could not do both effectively, they continued to take pride in the growth of their custom lens division, which they could not serve effectively or profitably.

The organizations that determine their UCA, incorporate it into their mission, put their energy and resources into doing it well, and ensure that they prove it during every customer touch point are the organizations that excel.

The companies that fail to determine and stick with one primary UCA (remembering that you must be competitive at all three) are the organizations that seem to fail fastest, which Quantum Lenses did, filing Chapter 11 three years later. When you try to be everything to everybody you simply must fail, and don't kid yourself... your customers see it!

So what is *your* organization's Unique Competitive Advantage? Is it unclear? Are *you* unclear? When I work with clients to develop their strategic plans, this discussion is usually the one most animated. Rarely does the executive team agree on their UCA. Many view it from their own "silo" position within the organization (think of various departments in an organization as separate and independent grain silos). Sales thinks that the UCA should be Customer Intimacy; Operations thinks it's Operational Excellence; Information Technology believes it should be Product or Service Innovation. The key here is to decide what the customer has been led to expect from your overall organization *"after the sale."*

This is one of the most pivotal decisions your planning team will make and it impacts every other part of the planning process. Once again, follow the 80/20 rule and simplify. Be clear about what you are and what you aren't. Where do you have the best chance to succeed vs. your competition? Place your bets and your resources there.

Once they have determined their UCA, many of my clients have created inspirational, compelling and meaningful mission statements. Here are just a few:

- *We offer innovative solutions to anyone who has an office!*
- *Superior engineered materials... impeccable support.*
- *We are the creative provider of personalized, hand-crafted automotive car interior solutions.*
- *We are revolutionizing medicine using stem cells to enable drug discovery and life-changing therapies.*

Your mission statement can make all the difference between focused success and unfocused failure. You can decide to choose.

Step 4: Your Values – These are your ethics or code of the road. Your values are the rules that you want your people to follow as they work to achieve your vision and mission.

You can use your values to create an exciting and consistent culture if you are willing to attract to your organization and celebrate those who demonstrate your values. You must also have the courage not to hire and to sanction existing employees who don't.

Decide which five values are most important to you, your team's success and to your UCA. Invent your own or work with your team to craft them, but be sure to define what each one means so there is no room for interpretation. These are a few samples taken from hundreds of business plans my clients have created over the years – what are yours?

- **Teamwork** – Success is a collective effort with the focus on the overall team achieving its goals.
- **Dependability** – Our clients, employees and everyone we do business with can count on us to consistently do what we say we are going to do.
- **Integrity** – We uphold the highest moral, ethical and professional standards and honor our word in all our relationships.
- **Accountability** – Committed to performance and results, we set clear, measurable goals and consistently monitor progress to ensure that they are achieved.

- *Initiative* – We view problems as opportunities, and we go the extra mile to find ways to help our clients and our company to be successful.
- *Quality* – We are committed to being excellent at what we do.
- *Respect for Others* – We respect diversity and recognize people for the unique contributions that they bring.
- *Professionalism* – We conduct ourselves within the highest standards of conduct, responsiveness, approach and style.
- *Fun* – We will enjoy our efforts and will make a point of motivating each other to share a fun work environment.
- *Excellence* – We're not satisfied with good enough; we want to be the very best. We have high standards, work to exceed expectations, and always explore ways to do things better and more creatively.
- *Entrepreneurialism* – We value the business as our own and constantly look for ways to grow it.

Once you determine the top five values that will form the cornerstone of your culture, you must make sure that they *live* throughout your organization. *Don't just put your values on a plaque in the lobby or send them out to the team in some form of writing.* That isn't good enough if you want the rules to be embraced and to become part of your company's culture.

If you are serious about their importance, you can include a 360 evaluation of his or her demonstration of these values in each employee's performance review. The "360" refers to 360 degrees in a circle with the individual figuratively in the center of the circle, as visualized below.

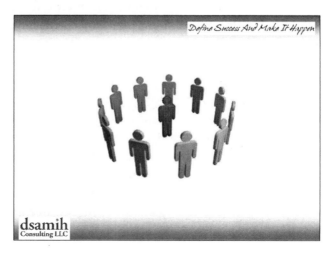

A 360 evaluation allows the individual to receive candid feedback from his or her manager, peers and subordinates through a quick, easy and anonymous survey. Having explicit, well-communicated values with clear definitions that are celebrated and enforced with colleague feedback can help you create a healthy organizational culture that attracts the talent you need to achieve your plans and one that is much easier to manage.

Step 5: Your Top 5 Success Metrics – These are the numbers we talked about in the DSAMIH chapter that you will track to monitor progress toward the plan outlined above. You probably measure a lot of things at your company. How do you decide what the top *five* metrics should be?

Picture this… Have you ever visited a patient in the intensive care unit? Not a pleasant experience, I know. But over the bed is a monitoring board that tracks vital signs or those measures of the human body that indicate healthy body functioning. There are thousands of measures of the human body that *aren't* on that board (red blood cell count, white blood cell count, cholesterol, weight) although the technology is available to have most of them up there. Why aren't these metrics included? Because the doctor doesn't want all those numbers on the screen. He or she wants to see at a glance whether the patient is alive and thriving, alive and deteriorating, or gone! Too many numbers on the board would make it difficult to monitor the most essential issues for that patient. Yet if one of those numbers goes south, the doctor will go deeper and collect more information on that number.

The same is true of your company. Your organization measures a lot of things. In fact, some of my clients measure everything that moves! So which numbers are the ones most important to your success? That's the key question.

I often ask the executive teams I work with to imagine that the vision we've just created actually happened in the period of time for which we were planning. I ask them to imagine that in order to celebrate, the leader decides to go on a vacation with his family, chartering a small plane to take them to a beautiful island destination in the Caribbean. Unfortunately, the plane crashes on a tiny deserted island somewhere on the way. The good news? Everyone on the plane is fine – no one suffers even a scratch. They have a supply of food and water for a year and they even have their favorite beverages!

Our leader is pretty happy out there with his family and his umbrella drinks, but because he is going to be stuck there for a year, eager to know how his company is doing, he asks his direct reports to charter a plane to fly-by once a month (okay, so you'll have to suspend your disbelief here). These direct reports are instructed to fly over the leader's island with a banner streaming behind the plane that has only five numbers on it. Not spreadsheets, not financial reports, not lengthy sentences... only five numbers. Which five numbers would he want to see on that banner so he could know that his company is still thriving?

In executive planning sessions, I ask this question of the leader's team. With the DSAMIH process, the leader is initially not permitted to answer the question about which five numbers would be ideal. His or her team is tasked to respond and their answers are usually out of the box, silo-focused and too numerous for that banner!

Not all the most important numbers or success metrics they mention are dollars. Most teams think that the leader wants to see something around revenue and profit or EBITDA, but they also think he or she needs numbers around employee productivity, throughput, growth of specific products/services/lines, sales pipeline, client satisfaction, accounts receivable, employee satisfaction, quality, etc. The list is endless. The art is to determine the top five measurable drivers of the company's success for that year and for that plan period.

We then use a process to narrow the 20 or 30 success metrics the team frequently offers up to those which they collectively consider the top five most important in *priority order*. Remember, this is just the team's point of view. The leader has yet to weigh in. What an enlightening way for the leader to learn what the team thinks is truly most important! If the team is right and they have made all the appropriate decisions without being directed, they now *own* the plan, which is ideal. If the leader feels that the team is off base in some area it is now the leader's golden opportunity to educate, inform and redirect.

By the way, these top five success metrics usually equate to what the leader wants the rest of the organization to pay most attention to (note the organizational triangle concept from the *DSAMIH* chapter). If the five numbers chosen don't meet this litmus test of organizational focus, we stay and debate them until they do.

Ken, the CEO of Doctor's Hospital, a large medical center in the Northwest, had arranged for me to facilitate a two-day planning session with his team using the process described above. Ken's team had determined their SWOT, vision, mission and values. After much animated discussion, they determined that their Unique Competitive Advantage was Customer Intimacy. They had ambitious plans for growth and now it was time to outline their top five success metrics. In my discussions with him prior to the planning session, Ken thought that the success metrics would be financially driven and would look something like this:

1. Day's Cash on Hand
2. Profit Margin
3. Patient Satisfaction
4. Salaries as a % of Revenue
5. Net Revenue per Weighted Patient Day

After going through the planning process and then listening to his direct reports arrive at *their* prioritized list that follows, Ken had to agree that they were right!

1. Patient Satisfaction
2. Employee Satisfaction
3. % Compliance with Core Quality Measures
4. # Inter-Campus Transfers
5. Profit

Ken and his team collectively came to understand that if their UCA was Customer Intimacy, patient satisfaction would be the biggest driver of their success over the three year period for which they were planning. They realized that they wanted every "triangle" in their organization to be focused and measured on their contributions to this first metric. They also came to realize that if patient satisfaction scores were to improve, employees needed to feel valued and empowered, thus the new metric #2 was created.

Metric #3 would get everyone focused on the quality of medical care delivered, as measured by a formula that would include several essential components of care quality.

They also determined that if they failed to collaborate with and earn referrals or transfers from other smaller feeder hospitals in the area, they would not achieve the volume of admissions required to be financially successful, so metric #4 was created.

And finally, they focused their layers of triangles on what they could do, beyond the above, to achieve metric #5, understanding that if they were successful with the top four metrics that profit would surely follow.

What are the key metrics that will drive your organization's success? That is where you want to place your bets (your staff, time, money and resources). Rather than just assuming that your top metrics are revenue and profit and that everyone will know what they need to do to achieve both, can you determine exactly what you want each person in the organization to focus on that will help you achieve your financial goals?

Doctor's Hospital did and they did it well. But before they could cascade the goals and ask everyone in the organization what their individual contributions would be to these key metrics or drivers, they needed to be specific about what the organization's goal targets were.

So once we know our top five success metrics in priority order, we must project where each of these metrics needs to be by year for the next three to five years in order to achieve the vision, after which we break the current year into monthly targets so as to have a shorter-term accountability tool. It is not worthwhile to establish monthly targets beyond the next 12 months, as long as we know what those annual milestones are.

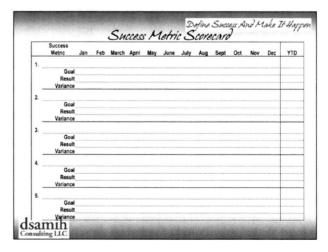

As you plot your monthly targets, don't divide by 12, but rather look historically at how these numbers are likely to come in over a year's time. Remember that every year has its cycles and seasonality. Using a success metric spreadsheet like the one above, plot the targets for each of your top five goals as realistically as you can to ensure meaningful accountability. Consider improving over time and ramping up your goal targets over the course of the year.

Step 6: Your Top 10 Initiatives – These are the top 10 action steps that must be accomplished in order to achieve this plan.

Once Ken's team at Doctor's Hospital had completed their SWOT, vision, mission, values and top five success metrics, they revisited each to decide what specifically they would do to make them happen. They revisited their top three weaknesses, opportunities and threats, deciding specifically what to do about each, who would do it and when it would get done.

They reviewed their Unique Competitive Advantage and mission. They then decided what they had to do to support that mission with both their marketing efforts and brand management, outlining who would do it and when would get done. They were also gratified to realize that by defining their top five success metrics and preparing to cascade them through the organization that they were already going a long way to make their agreed upon UCA and mission live in the organization.

They reviewed the vision and success metric goal targets that they had agreed upon as a team, deciding what they must do differently to achieve this success. Who would do it and when would it get done?

They put all their decisions into the following format assigning only one ultimately accountable party and a specific due date for each.

Who	What	When

They prioritized all of their potential action steps into the top 10 that would most move the needle toward planned success. Are these the only 10 things their organization would do that year? Of course not. But these are the 10 that they all agreed were most important to success and which must not slip through the cracks. They agreed to monitor progress monthly.

I find that it is consistently possible to accomplish 10 important, clearly defined initiatives in a year. Deploy resources to those action steps that are most important. These *will* get done because that is where your entire team's focus lies. Then you can start on a few more. Doctor's Hospital was amazed at how much they got done in a year with this kind of focus and discipline.

Step 7: Budgets – Ken and his team then created an annual budget based on the above decisions and solely on those decisions. This eliminated the typical dysfunctional corporate process of asking each department to determine its budget in a silo, based on its own interpretation of what will happen the next year. This kind of budgeting process usually results in a large consolidated expense total that the CFO can only react to with a heart attack or with angry direction for everyone to cut their budgets by 20% across the board. You've been there, haven't you? Avoid the insanity and let your carefully crafted business plan decisions drive and inform your budget process.

Step 8: Cascade goals and negotiate success metrics – Once the top triangle at Doctor's Hospital knew it's top five success metrics in priority order and knew what its monthly and annual goal targets were, it could align the goals for each of its teams throughout the organization using the cascading triangle process described in the *DSAMIH* chapter. So success metrics were negotiated by the leader of each triangle with each member of his or her team using the following questions:

"Now that you know the overall company direction (vision) and how we will measure success as an organization:

1. What are *your* best contributions, and
2. How can we measure *your* success?"

Ken and his team had to be ready to push through resistance when a team member inevitably said, "I'm so busy and have so many responsibilities that my job just can't be measured!" *I reminded them that I have personally negotiated success metrics with over 2,500 senior executives from CEOs to executives in sales, operations, finance, human resources and information services, and haven't yet found a job that can't be objectively measured.*

> **Without objective measures people simply cannot be effectively held accountable.**

As the employees of Doctor's Hospital made determinations about their most valuable contributions, the leaders of each triangle asked them to evaluate their responses against the following clear criteria for effective success metrics:

- *Do they define your best contributions to the success of the team?*

- *Are they within your sphere of influence?* Success metrics must be able to be controlled or influenced by you. But be careful! No one in the organization is in 100% control of anything. You have to convince, cajole and persuade others over whom you have no reporting authority to do things in order for you to be successful. Not even your president/CEO has 100% control. Don't demand that you have 100% control over the metric in order to establish your goal. If you had full control, the goal would be too small to be worthy of you. Take a risk. Be willing to play the champion role. Take responsibility, when appropriate, to spearhead or influence to completion, a critical process through the organization.

- *Are the success metrics attainable yet challenging?* Some employees like to establish pie-in-the-sky metrics – goals so sexy that everyone agrees that they would be wonderful if achieved. But pie-in-the-sky metrics won't be appreciated by your team or by the organization. They simply don't happen, and someone else will be required pick up the slack. Here's a pie-in-the-sky example: "I will achieve a 90% customer satisfaction rating by January 1!" This is an unreasonable metric if your current customer satisfaction rating is 60% and it is now November. The metric sounds great, but it is clearly not achievable.

Why do people suggest such metrics? Because there is no way anyone would hold them accountable to that goal. This is just another way to sound important while escaping real accountability.

But we don't want sandbag goals either and as we've already learned, we can use team negotiation and peer pressure to avoid these types of goals.

- *Are they measurable rather than action steps?* Remember that success metrics have numbers and due dates. Action steps outline how you are going to get there.

- *Are they in alignment with your manager and with each other?* If not, stay and keep negotiating until they are in alignment.

- *Do they aggregate to the overall organization's success metrics from Step 5 above?* If not, stay and keep negotiating until they do.

Once negotiated, the hospital leaders had each team member complete his/her own success metric spreadsheet like the one we used for the overall organization:

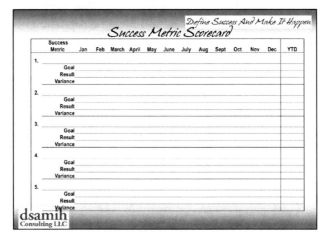

They then committed to holding themselves accountable with an *MIH (Make It Happen)* meeting each month! They ensured that each team member measured and published to their team where they were against their monthly and year-to-date goals. As explained in the *DSAMIH* chapter, they used the best advice of the team to decide what they would do differently to achieve any goal for which they were behind.

The result of all this planning? Ken and Doctor's Hospital increased profits by over 60% in a three-year period, far surpassing their business plan goals while becoming the largest, most profitable hospital in the network. Ken was promoted to Corporate VP and Doctor's Hospital became the role model for all their affiliate hospitals. All because they took a few days to decide what success looked like, identify their key business drivers, negotiate measurable goals throughout the organization in alignment with their definition of success and then report on those goals monthly.

DSAMIH Consulting offers a simple process for using the best ideas of the executive team in a truly collaborative way to create this entire eight-step plan *in only two days*, generating a concise 15-20 page PowerPoint plan that is easily communicated to and understood by everyone in the organization. What follows are some basic Do's and Don'ts that I have learned from this process that if followed, will allow you to create powerful, no-stress plans for your organization:

Do's and Don'ts for Effective Business Planning

What if the company you work for doesn't have a vision or hasn't communicated it?

DON'T wait for your manager to tell you the "Plan." DON'T ask your managers in the hallway what your goals or success metrics are. (They will look like deer in the headlights if you do.)

DO create a plan with your direct reports that reflects your best understanding of the company's future and your department's role in that future. Float that plan up to your manager. Give him or her something to react to so you can learn if you are going in the right direction. Use the assumptive close: "Fred, what do you think of this plan? Are we in alignment with your vision of the future? My team is going 100 miles an hour in this direction, so please let me know if we need to change course!" Fred will be amazed with your clarity, insight and initiative.

Who should write the plan?

DON'T write this plan yourself and hope for your team or your organization to follow you. It will become your plan only, and others will have no opportunity to share their important perspectives or feel ownership of the plan. If you write this plan single-handedly I guarantee that it will fizzle.

DO include your direct reports and develop the plan together. Use everyone's best thinking.

Who should run the planning session?

DON'T conduct this planning session yourself; you need to be a participant rather than a facilitator. Otherwise, people will tend to defer to your view, which will shut down the healthy debate and creative thinking essential to effective planning.

DO have an unbiased facilitator who can:

1. Pull the best ideas from the team
2. Involve and engage everyone on the team
3. Shut down discussion when it goes off the reservation
4. Stop those who want to grandstand their ideas
5. Allow you to teach and redirect when necessary
6. Help you arrive at clear, prioritized, actionable decisions, and
7. Help you all have fun in the process and get it all completed in two days!

If you are too small or can't afford a planning facilitator, consider bringing in an objective strategic thinker from your network of friends and colleagues – someone with no internal bias who can help you maneuver through the process outlined in this chapter. Just be sure to let the person know what his or her role will be (per the above seven bullets) and determine whether he or she is willing and able to play that role.

How long and detailed should the plan be?

DON'T create a plan that has "thud factor." Avoid small type, thick notebooks and wordy descriptions. Plans with great thud factor fizzle every time because no one but the typist reads them. These types of plans are loaded with verbs and descriptors rather than measurable outcomes (i.e., "We will dominate our markets! We will eliminate waste! We will create loyal customers! We will be the best!").

These kinds of statements might sound terrific, but they are completely ineffective in a business plan. They are fluffy and unnecessary. What do they mean anyway? How will you know when you've gotten there? You won't. And what will people on your team say when you ask them if they have accomplished the plan? "Of course I have!" will be their response. But how can you feel good about that response when the goals in the plan are so poorly and unclearly described? I challenge you to review your *last* business plan and check for the amount of flowery language that cannot be measured with clear outcomes.

DO make your plan clear, concise and actionable. I believe in using PowerPoint for business plans with large type, lots of space and no more than 15-20 pages. If you can't explain your organization's vision in that amount of space, you truly don't understand it yourself, and neither will anyone else on the team. It is difficult to achieve clarity, but...

> ## Clarity is the friend of accountability!

Clarity is required to make progress. Reduce words, bumper sticker your thoughts and focus on actionable measures, deliverables and due dates. My clients find that this is not only easier, clearer and more rewarding, but results improve! And who doesn't love that?

How should you spend your time during the planning session?

DON'T spend your executive team's precious time word-smithing mission statements or values definitions.

DO get the gist of what is important to the team and have the facilitator do the word-smithing later. I have seen high-level executives spend a whole day on a 10-word mission statement. Your mission will be highly impactful in your organization, but it is not the highest and best use of your team to spend a full day word-smithing a bumper sticker. Let the facilitator do the work and give you something to react to and finalize so that all agree it is clear and compelling.

Once the plan is complete, to whom should you communicate it?

DON'T keep it to yourselves hoping everyone else in the organization will figure the plan out on their own. DON'T worry that you are giving your people too much information and that they will use it against you or give it to the competition.

DO share the plan with anyone in your organization who will help you achieve it. (By the way, that is everyone!) Let them know that you have a plan, so they can trust that you know where you are going and so they can determine what their contributions should be. Let me put this in perspective…

Have you ever driven somewhere and been dependent on the passenger for directions? Would you prefer that the passenger give you those directions by yelling at you each time you miss a turn or by giving you general directions up front, outlining specific turns before those turns are required? Of course you'd prefer the latter. So would the people in your organization!

Tell them what you know so they can make informed decisions. Don't assume they know what's in your head and then chastise them for not following your lead. Be explicit about where you are going and what they can do to help you get there. Give them the road map so they can help you succeed. Your business plan is the road map for the team so you can stop yelling at them at every missed turn.

DO share this plan with your Board, advisors, investors and/or bank. Let them know that you know exactly where you're going and that your entire team knows what they must do to get there. Let them measure your performance through the updated monthly success metric scorecard for your company. Your meetings will be much more focused and positive.

Creating an effective business plan with clear vision, mission, values and success metrics is an energizing and empowering experience for your team. It will take a little thought and time, but if you use the basic process outlined above, you can enjoy the power of crafting your results rather than reacting to your markets, without spending exorbitant time and resources on the planning effort.

Leaders who take the time to build and communicate concise, effective plans, win out over their competitors every time. You can do it too.

Summary and Action Steps:

- Decide that you do have the power to craft your company/division/department's future.
- Follow the eight-step process to dream big and be clear on what success looks like:
  Step 1: Situation or SWOT Analysis
  Step 2: Your Vision
  Step 3: Your Mission

Step 4: Your Values
Step 5: Your Top five Success Metrics
Step 6: Your Top 10 Initiatives
Step 7: Budgets
Step 8: Cascade goals and negotiate success metrics
- Report on your success metrics monthly to your team
- Build an accountability system. Record your results.
- Celebrate your successes and then create a new vision!

Planning – the Bumper Sticker – from Lewis Carroll: If you don't know where you're going, any road will get you there.

4

Secret 3 – Compelling Life Plans in Just 4 Hours!

How YOU can be the author of your career and your life

How much influence do you have over your own life? I suggest that you have more than you might realize. Not convinced? Then think about this…

Imagine that you are going on vacation. Would you just hop in a car and start driving? Or would you weigh your vacation options, determine your destiny, plot your route and perhaps make some flight or hotel arrangements in advance? That's right. You would do the latter. Why? Because vacation time is precious. You don't want to waste a moment of it being lost, confused or inconvenienced. You want everything to go smoothly so you can enjoy the most of every moment.

Do vacation plans ever go awry? All the time. Flights get cancelled, hotels go through unexpected renovations and tours get missed. So why bother planning when all these variables can go wrong? The answer is easy. Without proper planning, you have a significantly reduced chance of enjoying your vacation. When plans go wrong, you can recover. However, without those plans you tend to drift through every day at the mercy of what just happens to you.

It's the same with life. Most of us spend more time planning our vacations than we do our lives or careers. Imagine taking the approach we just described in the last chapter for planning your business and applying it to your life. Do you remember the eight-step planning process? Let's look at it this time from a personal life-planning perspective:

Eight Steps to Crafting the Perfect Plan for your Life

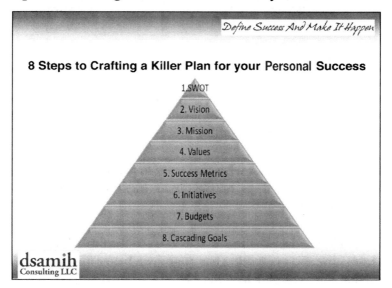

Define Success And Make It Happen

8 Steps to Crafting a Killer Plan for your Personal Success

1. SWOT
2. Vision
3. Mission
4. Values
5. Success Metrics
6. Initiatives
7. Budgets
8. Cascading Goals

dsamih
Consulting LLC

Step 1: Situation or SWOT Analysis – Know your starting points. These are your Strengths, Weaknesses, Opportunities and Threats. It is critical not only to know what they are but to know your personal top three in each category.

Spend some time thinking through your best gifts, your lesser strengths, your opportunities and barriers. Are you unsure what they are? Ask the people closest to you. Collect a list and narrow it down. Be clear and objective about your current situation. Consider initiating a 360 evaluation in which your manager, peers and subordinates can give you honest, *anonymous* feedback about both your greatest strengths and lesser strengths. Anyone who has known you for more than a day or two, not only *knows* what they are, but they talk about them in the coffee room! Wouldn't *you* like to know what they are?

As we work through the personal life planning process, we'll study Samantha's story. Samantha was a high-powered, successful VP at a Northern California design firm. Concerned about some feedback they were getting about her, her company asked her to participate in one of my two-day leadership workshops, during which she received 360 feedback from her manager, peers and subordinates. Her recurring 360 themes looked like this:

Strengths	Opportunities for Improvement
Charismatic	Controlling
Highest producer	Abrasive
Knows everybody in the industry	Self serving
Energetic ambition	

Samantha was eager to address her opportunities for improvement so she could achieve her ambitious goals, and asked me to help her with a life plan. Let's follow her journey through the planning process...

Step 2: Your Vision – This is what you want to get out of life in terms of your health, job, income, relationships, house, car, savings, travel, time spent and with whom that time is spent.

Decide what perfect looks like three to five years in the future. Imagine that it is five years from now and everything has gone even better than you could have hoped for. What does your life look like? How are you doing on all the areas listed above (i.e., health, job, income, etc.)?

Jot these words on a list and then write a sentence next to each one of those words, describing your perfect life in five years. And remember, as you visualize your future, when talking about health, don't say you want to avoid illness. Say that you want to have a blood pressure of 110/70 and a total cholesterol count below 200 by September of next year. When talking about income, rather than saying that you want don't want to worry about money, say that you want to have at least $XXXX in liquid savings by July of next year. It is amazing how turning our negative thoughts into positive, specific statements can affirm a brighter, healthier future.

Put this book down and give yourself some time to write your thoughts about each word: job, health, income, time spent and with whom, relationships, travel, house, car...

Once you are completely happy with your list – I warn you that this will be the difficult part – prioritize each line so that you know your top five priorities for the next five years. Know your number-one most important goal, your second, third, etc. They must be in priority order!

Your top priorities at 25 years of age are much different than they are at 40 or 50. There is no right answer. It isn't wrong to prioritize one thing over another, even when it's a tough call. You simply need to know what is right for you over this next five years. This important five-year prioritization helps to eliminate hours of angst over the daily and weekly competing pressures that hit us all. When you know your top five priorities for the next few years, the decisions about where to put your time become much easier.

Samantha had ambitious professional aspirations and hoped to run her own profit and loss division of the company. As we worked on her vision, she documented what perfect would look like in this new role in terms of increased influence in the organization, increased income and what it would feel like to be debt-free, have opportunities to work with creative people, and perhaps buy the perfect house. She also wanted to be more fit and to lose weight. As she visualized what each of these would look like, we were able to document her positive, measurable and specific goals that became her five-year vision.

As Jack Nicklaus has taught us, if you know where you are now (your SWOT) and you know where you're going (your vision), you can reverse engineer to determine what must be done by year to achieve that vision. But first, Samantha needed to determine her mission in life...

Step 3: Your Mission – This is a simple, compelling sentence that states who you are, why you are here and how you want to be remembered by the people you touch in your life. It is a lot to fit in to one concise bumper sticker, but if you are successful, this will be a statement of purpose that you can provide direction for a lifetime.

In order to create this statement for Samantha, I asked her to picture a scenario offered by Stephen Covey in *7 Habits of Highly Effective People*...

You are attending your own funeral. Imagine that at the end of your long, full life the legions of people you have touched will be standing up to say something about you. What do you want them to say? Get it down to a few compelling ideas and get that into a simple, clear, short sentence.

After several careful iterations, she wrote: *I will be remembered as a force of nature who improved the design industry and the lives I touched in the process.*

Once you have your mission statement, you need to reverse engineer. Ask yourself how you have to live your life so that this is what people will want to say about you when you are gone. Use your mission statement as an ongoing decision-making tool for your life.

My clients have created many inspirational personal missions over the years. Here are just a few more:

- *Those whose lives I touch will be better, stronger and happier because they knew me.*
- *I will be the kind of parent my kids want to become.*
- *People will say that they became their best selves because they knew me.*
- *I will be someone who adds joy to every situation.*
- *I will follow my dreams and kiss the rest good-bye!*
- *I will be remembered as someone who helped challenged children thrive in this world.*

Step 4: Your Values – These are your ethics or code of the road. These are the rules you want to follow as you work to achieve your vision and mission.

You can use these values to attract to you people who share your rules of conduct and opportunities that allow you to express them. If you don't know what your values are, you sometimes won't recognize the perfect fit when it shows up in your life. And it always does!

I have already offered sample values that *companies* have used, but personal values can also include words like personal responsibility, passion, integrity, autonomy, freedom and fun.

Choose your own descriptors and narrow them down to no more than five. These five values define those attributes most important to you in yourself, a friend, a colleague, a boss. Use them to proactively determine where and with whom you best fit. Define each in a short sentence so there is no room for interpretation.

If you are serious about the importance of your rules of conduct, ask questions about these five values to determine how your company, a potential friend, a potential colleague feels about them. Make your decisions accordingly about who to work for and with, who to befriend and with whom you should spend time.

After careful consideration, Samantha outlined *her* personal values as follows:

Integrity – I value people who consistently do the right thing, regardless of whose interest is served.

Excellence – I am not satisfied with good enough; I want to be the very best. I have high standards, work to exceed expectations, and always explore ways to do things better and more creatively.

Accountability – I am responsible for my actions and I follow through.

Passion – I have fun and enjoy what I do.

Creativity – I love to create "unique."

Now that Samantha had completed her SWOT, vision, mission and values, we needed to know how we would measure her success...

Step 5: Your Top five Success Metrics – These are the numbers you will track that will best monitor progress toward the life you have planned. How can you measure a life? What numbers would you put on the "life banner" streaming behind your plane?

This isn't as difficult as you might think. Take a look at your vision statement from Step 2 above that outlines your top five most important priorities for the next five years. How can you measure your progress on each?

Is some kind of health goal in your top five? If so, you could measure your weight, percent body fat (I hate that one!), cholesterol count, blood pressure, number of medications, number of one-hour workouts per week or number of miles run each month. These are just some of many useful success metrics for health. What are yours?

Is there an income or savings goal in your top five? You could measure progress by the number of your business goals achieved (which link to income), savings achieved monthly, a manager's monthly score from 1 to 5, offering her perception of how well you are accomplishing your business success metrics.

Is there a relationship goal? These can be measured by the number of dinners at home with your family each week, the number of your kids' special events missed, the number of date nights you have each month with your spouse, the number of events you attend each month that offer you an opportunity to meet that "special someone," the number of times you receive an unsolicited "I love you" from your family and so on. Be creative but clear so that you will know when you are achieving your meaningful goals.

Project where each of these numbers need to be by year for the next five years to achieve your vision. Then, if you're really serious, break the current year into monthly targets not by dividing by 12, but rather looking at how these numbers are likely to come in over a year's time. If it's a weight goal, for example, consider improving it over time and ramping up your goal targets. Plot the targets as realistically as you can to ensure meaningful accountability.

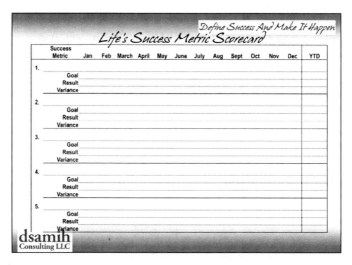

Hold yourself accountable each month! Write down where you are against your monthly and year-to-date success metrics. Decide what you will do differently to achieve any metric for which you are behind. You can even use this same spreadsheet that we used for your business plan!

Based on her vision, Samantha laid out the following prioritized success metrics and completed the above spreadsheet with her monthly and annual goal targets:

1. Number of milestones met on my project plan to have ultimate
    profit-and-loss responsibility at work. Note: She had listed about 50
    deliverables or milestones due over the course of a year, and simply
    plotted in each month's goal line, and the number of milestones due each
    month.
2. $ Income
3. $ Debt/Savings
4. # 1-hour Workouts
5. Weight

Now that we had her plan and how we were going to measure her success, we
needed to know how we were going to make it happen...

Step 6: Your Top Ten Initiatives – These are the top 10 action steps that
must be accomplished to achieve your plan.

Once you have completed the above steps, revisit your personal SWOT.
You determined your top three opportunities for improvement. Now decide
specifically what you will do about each and when each action step will be
accomplished.

Review your vision and your personal goal targets. What specifically must you
do differently to achieve this success? When will these steps be accomplished?

Go through each page of the plan and decide what must happen to be successful
– be specific – and decide what the results will look like. Don't write down what
you will *think*, but rather what you will *do*.

Put your action steps into the following format and note that the "Who" will be
you in most cases:

Who	What	When

Prioritize all of your potential action steps into the top 10 that will most move the
needle toward your vision. Specify 10 things you can do *this* year that will move

you toward your goal. Narrow your focus. Deploy your personal energy to that which is most important. With this level of focus and discipline these *will* get done!

As we began to build Samantha's initiatives, we really honed in on her strengths and weaknesses. She was grateful that people had acknowledged her strengths, but angry that so many people in her organization felt she was controlling, abrasive and self serving. What was wrong with *them*? I explained that when many people say the same thing about you, there is truth there, and that she must look carefully at that truth.

She went on to explain how the leadership of her design firm was incompetent, consistently making poor market decisions and treating their own people badly. She felt she needed to ignore their direction and do what *she* knew was truly required both internally and externally in order for the company to be successful. In fact, that was why she wanted responsibility for her own profit-and-loss division!

Yikes! No wonder she hadn't been promoted to the role she desired and was now receiving the kind of feedback she was. When you feel you can no longer respect or follow the leadership of your company, you have only three options: you can change yourself and genuinely accept and support your leadership, you can work within the system and company values to change it, or you can leave. It is never acceptable to choose your own path, disregard your leaders and continue to collect a paycheck from them.

Long story short, Samantha used her personal life plan just as we built it to form her *own* successful design company which attracted the kind of projects she wanted to be part of and which allowed her to create her own reputation for creating unique and innovative commercial spaces. What is more, she achieved all of *her* success metrics over the next three years, and she did it her way!

Step 7: Budgets – You should have a personal budget and a family budget, which should now be based on the above decisions, which, of course, Samantha did so she could achieve her savings goal.

Step 8: Negotiate goals and success metrics – Do this with your family and/or significant others. But don't get so excited about the life plan you have just created that you go home to excitedly share *"Our* Plan" with *your* family. Ask your significant other to create his or her own, independent plan.

Compare notes. No two people will ever want exactly the same things. Find out where you have similar goals. Where do your goals differ? Determine what you can *each* do to help the other get what you both want and need. Successful marriages and relationships require ongoing and effective negotiation.

Use this process to energize your relationship. Calmly discuss any tensions that may arise from you and your significant other wanting different things. Brainstorm creatively about how you can *both* get what you want. Getting these issues out in the open and on the table can be one of the healthiest things you do to enhance your life together.

If your significant other is not the "life planning" type (mine isn't), don't harp or badger him or her into creating a plan. Explain that you would like to know what is most important to your loved one so you can work to help him or her achieve it. But if your mate would rather not go through the process or even discuss personal priorities, you can simply share yours and ask if there are any concerns or surprises in what they see. Offer support to your loved one for achieving whatever he or she might mention as important. Then ask for the support you need to accomplish your goals. Once you have clarity, you can negotiate so you both win.

Consider creating a family plan. Involving your children in a family vision, mission, values and goal-setting process is one of the most effective ways to teach your children early on that they have the power to craft their own lives.

Samantha didn't have a family at the time, but used her plan to communicate to friends and colleagues what she needed from them and why, and she easily enlisted their enthusiastic support in helping her make her plan happen.

I have worked with CEOs and business owners as well as engineers, salespeople, administrators, finance people and self-professed "tech-driven geeks" to define success for their own personal lives and then put in place specific steps to make it happen. Using the same simple process we worked through for their business, they were able to create exciting life plans with clear steps to achieve them. Listen to what some of them say about this process:

- "I pulled out my life plan a year later and was dumbfounded that I had already achieved it all!"
- "You said that the power was in knowing what you want and writing it down. I was skeptical, but now I believe!"

Building a personal life plan is an energizing and empowering experience. It takes a little thought and time, but doesn't your life deserve a little of your focused attention? Enjoy the power of *crafting* rather than *reacting* to your life.

The same planning principles outlined above work for organizations, lives and careers. My clients who have invested the time to build them have realized a 90% success rate in achieving their personal and professional dreams. You can achieve yours too.

Summary and Action Steps:

- Decide that you *do* have the power to craft your personal future.
- Follow the eight-step process to dream big and be clear on what success looks like:
  Step 1: Situation or SWOT Analysis
  Step 2: Your Vision
  Step 3: Your Mission
  Step 4: Your Values
  Step 5: Your Top Five Success Metrics
  Step 6: Your Top 10 Initiatives
  Step 7: Budgets
  Step 8: Enlisting the support of your loved ones
- Report on your success metrics monthly to yourself and to your family. Build an accountability system. Record your results.
- Celebrate your successes and then create a new vision!

Life Planning – the Bumper Sticker – You master your life when the voice of your inner vision is louder than all other voices.

5

Secret 4 - Holding People Accountable

The secret to doing it without being a jerk

Now that we have clear business plans, visions and success metrics that have been developed by the team, it is time to hold our people accountable to them. Several of my clients tell me that this is the single most difficult thing they have on their professional plates. Dave, a CEO I've coached for years, mentioned that he absolutely had to do something about holding Tim, his VP of Sales, accountable for poor results. He pledged to not let another week go by without having a serious heart-to-heart talk with Tim. I received a call from Dave that week on Friday at 3:00 p.m. with an embarrassed confession that he had not yet talked with Tim and that he was, in fact, scouring his desk for something that might be more important than meeting with him before the end of the day.

Why do leaders have such a hard time holding their people accountable? I've heard all the excuses. They don't want to be the bad guy. They don't want the person to feel bad. They don't want to ruin their weekends. They don't want them to cry, be in denial or argue that they indeed *are* doing well. They don't want their people to go on the offensive and blame the boss. These are all excuses leaders tell themselves to avoid confrontation.

One of the most chronic cases of not holding people accountable happened in a large, well-known company with a long history of loyalty to its employees. I was working with the executive team on a five-year strategic plan, during which we determined their top five success metrics. I asked who the ultimately accountable party would be for each metric. The CEO chose the first, the COO the second, the CIO the third, the CFO the fourth and when we got to the fifth, they all said collectively, "Give that one to the three S's."

"The three S's?" I asked. "Who are they?" They obviously weren't in the room.

The C-Group responded, "Susie, Sam and Sarah. They are our dead weight!"

Really? They had an acronym for their dead weight? Unfortunately, this happens more often than you might expect. Failure to hold people accountable is often caused by the "nice-guy" syndrome. Leaders tell themselves that they are putting up with poor performance out of loyalty to the employees, allowing them to maintain their jobs and incomes despite poor results. "Where else could they go?" they ask themselves.

You need to know that everyone can be an A-player somewhere. Leaders have an obligation to repair or replace, and they must act quickly if they are to be fair to the employee. Do you think this organization was doing the three S's any favors? How about the *other* employees? Do you think they knew about the dead-weight acronym? Do you think the three S's knew? Of course they did. I interviewed Sam and asked if he knew about the label. He looked down, nodded sadly and offered, "You have no idea how demoralizing it is coming in here every day knowing how they talk about us." I asked Sam why he continued to do it. He explained that he had been there so long that he didn't know what else to do.

Leaders can actually ruin people's futures by not holding them accountable. Help them get to a role either inside or outside the organization where they *can* excel. If you don't, you not only damage their futures, but the message you send to the rest of the team is that mediocrity is acceptable. Why should your talented staff go above and beyond to excel when there are people on the team who simply get by and still receive a paycheck?

In this chapter, you will learn how to hold your people accountable fairly and without stress every time using two basic components of accountability – process and personal coaching style. Let's start first with the process.

How to avoid "What do you mean I need to improve? I'm doing great!"

As outlined previously, all employees in the organization should know what the measurable goals or success metrics are that represent their best contributions to the overall plan. Without these measures, individual success lies in the eye of the beholder and is usually judged after the fact with subjective performance reviews. Performance evaluations should never be a surprise as they often are when based on the person's recent activities or the current mood of the manager.

The proactive determination of each person's most important contributions and how he or she will be measured are essential to effective accountability. Otherwise, the person being coached may simply and justifiably say, "You're wrong. I'm doing great!"

What Should People Be Held Accountable For?

Rick, CEO of a global hotel chain and a really nice guy, was frustrated that his employees around the world had come to expect "outstanding" performance reviews each year, feeling cheated if they received anything less. Of course, they also expected the higher merit increases that went with such reviews. He felt torn each year as he tried to deliver truthful, realistic employee feedback, while he worried that he might be perceived as an ungrateful or miserly leader.

So every year, his reviews held more and more superlatives and he felt pressure to increase the merit and bonus pool although the company's travel business had suffered in a down economy. He asked for my help in building performance reviews that were fair, objective and which reinforced the behaviors he most needed from his team.

Together, Rick and I built a performance review process for his company, specific to each position title, to ensure that *prior* to the beginning of the evaluation period, each employee would understand how they would be measured against each of the following six categories:

1. **The company's Mission Statement** – How well they demonstrated the hotel's mission.

2. **The company's Values** – How well they demonstrated the hotel's five company values.

3. **The top five Competencies required for success in this specific position** – How well they demonstrated the top competencies identified for each position. (This will be outlined in Chapter 6.)

4. **The *company's* overall success**, as measured by the hotel's top five success metrics, reported monthly with favorable variances highlighted in green and unfavorable variances highlighted in red. You will find this outlined in a sample company-level success metric spreadsheet below (you won't be able to see the red and green variation, but you get the idea.)

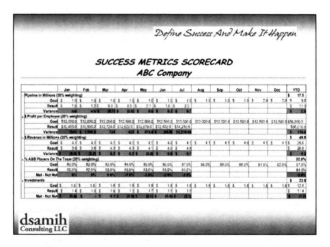

5. **The *individual's* success**, as measured by his or her top five success metrics, negotiated prior to the evaluation period with their team's triangle and reported monthly with favorable variances highlighted in green and unfavorable variances highlighted in red. For individual team members, you would use the same spreadsheet format as the overall company scorecard above.

6. Another option we made available to Rick's review process was a category for the ***individual's successful completion of specific Objectives*** as outlined proactively with project plan milestones,

due dates and budgets. (These are for those positions most focused on completion of various projects that don't have specific, monthly, measurable outcomes.)

Rick understood that each of these six bullets could and should be objectively measured specific to each position. Each should be weighted according to relative importance. ("Weighting" simply means the percentage that each goal represents to the individual's overall performance.) Rick's employees had to understand expectations so well that they could calculate at any time throughout the year how they were performing… an objective calculation which should then match their manager's at any given time.

All employees in the organization should know and care about the status of their numbers. All goals should be realistic. Employee compensation should be based on achievement of agreed-upon results rather than on activity or the manager's discretion.

When accountability is based on activity, discretion or long, wordy performance review forms that evaluate employees in subjective ways not tied to their own specific contributions and results, you will find that you have "high graders" and "low graders" among your management team. The high graders will write enthusiastic, emotional and articulate justifications for high performance reviews and large increases. And they will sound good. The low graders will write less, measure everyone about the same, or may not evaluate the employee at all. Neither approach is fair to the employee or to the organization.

The bottom line is that if you base performance and compensation on anything other than results, you create a highly charged political environment that breeds entitlement and rewards sycophancy, while at the same time reducing the return on investment from your essential human capital.

After we negotiated clear goals or success metrics for every employee in the hotel using the cascading *Defining Success* process, and each person knew how their performance reviews would be calculated, it was time to *Make It Happen or* inspect what we expected.

How Should Employees Be Held Accountable? Follow Seven Simple MIH Steps

If like Rick, you prefer to avoid confrontation, I'll show you how to let the *MIH (Make It Happen)* accountability process work for *you*. These are the seven easy steps I facilitated with Rick and his team to run these monthly meetings so they actually worked!

1. *MIH Meetings – Organizing your triangle*

Rick met monthly with his direct reports. He did not invite members of the Board to join these meetings. These were Rick's meetings! He needed to create a safe environment with healthy debate that allowed him to surface and resolve obstacles to his team's goals. If his Board had been there, his direct reports would have directed their comments to them and it would have become the *Board members'* meeting.

Rick's direct reports were to take full responsibility for the goals they had negotiated with him and with *their* peers in that top triangle. However, I explained to them, "If you cannot resolve an obstacle critical to the success of the triangle that reports to you, then you have an obligation to surface that issue during the MIH meeting with Rick and your peer triangle so you can use their experience to resolve the obstacle." This allowed Rick to keep a "finger on the pulse" of the organization and to be informed early of barriers to success without having to connect with all layers of the organization or attend every layer's meetings.

2. *Meeting monthly*

Rick used these sessions to review the top five success metrics for each direct report. He scheduled these monthly sessions a year in advance and *after* the hotel's financials were available, so everyone could report *real* results. The team needed to be armed with the latest numbers in order to populate their latest month's results.

Why did I ask him to schedule these meetings a year in advance? Think about those individuals who might not want to attend accountability meetings. You can probably imagine that the employees who were consistently *not* hitting their goals were less than enthusiastic about the process. The peer pressure was a little uncomfortable, and late notice of a meeting would be a perfect excuse for such folks to have other plans.

Rick explained to his team that he was committed to reviewing the status of each team member's five most important individual contributions monthly and that they must, therefore, schedule around these important dates a year in advance. Was there anything more important? They had to agree there was not.

Why meet monthly? You will find that when you are monitoring the progress of each team member's top five metrics, if you allow too much time to pass before team review, you miss the opportunity for early interventions that allow you to catch and resolve problems early. Quarterly and semi-annual meetings are simply not frequent enough to ensure the successful execution of your vision and success metrics. Even if *some* metrics can only be measured quarterly most can be measured monthly, and you need to maintain a consistent monthly discipline if you are to create real accountability among the team.

Rick experienced three unforeseen but welcome outcomes from implementing the *MIH* accountability method:

- He was able to eliminate other regular and less productive meetings that were held to react to problems rather than to deal with them proactively
- He eliminated a weekly communication meeting with his direct reports designed to listen to irrelevant updates and to chase activity rather than receive updates on real results
- His stress level dropped dramatically. Why? Because he had been guilty of the following...

**The fastest road to burnout and failure
is chasing activity rather than results.**

---

3. *Giving them the big picture*

The first agenda item for these accountability meetings was for Rick to review the overall organization's success metric scorecard. You may feel uncomfortable about sharing company information with your team, especially if you are a private company, but you must share with them as much information as you can so they can make decisions within a framework of objective understanding. They must see how their efforts are affecting overall company results.

Have you ever walked into your office first thing in the morning and discovered a depressing report outlining stomach-lurching bad news about the company yet you can see clueless employees chatting amiably over coffee and having a great time? Share the pain! They should know exactly where the company stands as well as what they might do specifically to help.

Have you ever found a great report on your desk that shows the positive results of hitting a home run with your biggest client? Share that, too!

The more Rick's employees knew and understood about what was really happening in the organization, the more they owned their part in making the hotel's goals happen. Rick worried that they would want to claim their share of big bottom-line numbers. I explained that he had an obligation to teach them to think like business owners. Profits are required for investment back into the company and for the sustainability of employee jobs; these are not dollars that just go into the owners' pockets. Rick helped his employees understand that they must help ensure ongoing profits if the company was to grow and their jobs were to remain secure.

4. *I'll show you mine if you show me yours!*

We had each team member then present their success metric scorecard to their team triangle with favorable variances highlighted in green and unfavorable results in red. To avoid killing trees, we projected the completed sheets on screen rather than handing out hard copies. All direct reports had access to every team member's results.

We didn't have each team member simply *read* his or her numbers to the team – anyone can read and that makes for a truly boring meeting. Rather, we expected them to be prepared to talk about how they achieved success when the results were green and to outline a clear diagnosis for any result in red. For any goal not met, they had to reduce the problem to a bumper sticker question posed to their teammates and jot down all the suggestions offered, ultimately determining the two or three actions to which they would actually commit along with a due date for completion. For added accountability and reference, these collective individual commitments were documented and distributed to the entire team.

These meetings had relevance, conflict and resolution – the kind of stuff good books and movies are made of... unlike the boring communication meetings they had held in the past.

5. *Holding celebrations and rallies*

When goals were achieved, we celebrated team members' successes and asked them how they achieved them, thus sharing best practices.

When goals were missed it wasn't time for retribution, public humiliation or reprimand. This was a time to rally the team's best thinking around the obstacle so we could surface solutions. We kept all discussions positive. We ensured that the team focused discussion on what they *could* do – not what they *couldn't* do. We focused on how we could achieve success for everyone both as a team and as individuals rather than through competition with each other. Everyone can and should win. This isn't a fight for each one's piece of the pie, but rather it is a team effort to grow the size of the pie!

6. *Being clear that accountability is not negotiable*

It was made clear that this process would not go away – we pushed past any resistance. Those who consistently failed to make their own negotiated goals and didn't listen to the advice of their teams sometimes hated the process and tried to avoid the meetings. I advised Rick that if he got a call the morning of the *MIH* session from Sharon, a frequent offender, explaining that she was ill and wouldn't be able to make the meeting, that he should not reschedule the session. Rather than reward her avoidance, he would ask her to email her updated success metric spreadsheet in time for the meeting so her results could be reviewed as always.

Again, we used the process as the "bad guy." Because of the process, Rick didn't have to be like Dave, scouring his desk for something more important to do than discussing poor performance with an employee. No one in the organization escaped a team review of that which everyone had agreed were his/her most important contributions.

Sharon, who could not avoid the monthly meetings and who was not up to the task of succeeding in her given position actually "de-selected" herself to avoid the pressure of monthly reporting. She wasn't blind. She could see the writing on the wall, knew she was failing and chose to go to another company that didn't inspect what they expected. There she could be more successful.

Is it okay with you if people who consistently fail to contribute to your organization decides on their own to go to the competition? It seemed like a double win to Rick!

7. *What if they don't de-select?*

In the past, Rick would get into trouble with Human Resources (HR) when had tried all he knew how to do, had seen no improvement with a poor performer and angrily demanded HR's support in firing them *immediately*! Of course, when HR pulled the last performance review and it said that the employee was outstanding with no room for improvement, it made Rick's demand seem unfair, unreasonable and, frankly, illegal.

Suppose that Sharon hadn't de-selected on her own to go to the competition. With the *MIH* Accountability process, Rick had at his disposal:

- Documented goals that Sharon herself had negotiated with her team.
- Monthly results she had completed on her own all on one page that showed lots of red for unfavorable results, even after receiving monthly support and advice from her team.

Is there any better ammunition for progressive disciplinary action and potential termination? HR loved Rick's diligence and documentation!

Rick let the process work for him. He took it down through all layers of the organization to ensure alignment and accountability.

The end result for the hotel after Rick's upfront work on the performance review process, individual goal setting and monthly MIH meetings?

- The review process was less about his and his managers' "generosity" and more about how each employee actually performed.

- Compensation was based on pre-negotiated goals and results only, taking away all the pressure managers faced to either deliver "bad news" at performance review time or over-reward poor performers.
- Overall employee productivity rose by 17% or $2,000 in profit per employee.
- The amount paid out in increases and bonuses stayed about the same, but some made significantly less and others made significantly more, all based on real results.

Isn't this the kind of ownership, empowerment and responsibility you want *your* employees to have? With a little forethought, you can do this for *your* team and enjoy the enhanced communication, interaction and team building among your direct reports that will cause your results to soar. And you won't have to be like Dave, looking for an excuse to avoid talking to a poor performer. Such "talks" are built into the monthly team meetings!

Managing your A, B, C Players and On-Board Terrorists – another part of the accountability *process*

Recognize that in all organizations you have people who fall into each of the following categories:

Define Success And Make It Happen

A-B-C Player Evaluation

		Results?	
		Yes	No
VALUES?	Yes	A Players	B Players
	No	OBTs	C Players

dsamih
Consulting LLC

As you can see from the above quadrants, employees who get results and demonstrate the values are your A-players. They generate 80% of the productivity and rarely get much of your attention.

Employees who don't get results and don't follow your values are C-players. They consume 80% of managerial time and rarely become A or B players. You have an obligation with these folks to repair or replace. If these poor performers cannot change their behaviors you should initiate progressive disciplinary action.

The employees who are trying their hardest to fit into the culture and to be part of the team yet just aren't getting the desired results – these are your B-players who deserve coaching to better performance through the *Make It Happen (MIH)* process.

Employees who achieve results but don't follow your values are what we call On-Board Terrorists (OBTs). Not a politically correct label, but you get the idea. OBTs come to your meetings and appear to agree with your direction, but fully intend to go off in their own direction anyway. They achieve their numbers, but often at the expense of the rest of the team. The net effect of an OBT is a drain to your organization, because they diminish the productivity of those around them. Sound familiar? Samantha, who had opted to ignore the direction of her leaders in the last chapter was becoming an OBT. Do you have some in your organization?

Companies consistently have the most difficulty dealing with OBTs. Why? Because these people are pulling in the numbers! They are sometimes your best producers and often your prima donnas. However, when organizations look the other way for such employees, the message they send to the rest of the team is that the values don't really matter.

By the way, there are methods to hold people accountable to the values, but calling someone in your organization an On Board Terrorist is not one of them! I'm afraid this is a lawsuit waiting to happen. I use the phrase only to illustrate the point. However, you can let someone know that he or she has received a low values score on an objective performance evaluation, and that the person will have to improve that score in order to retain employment in your organization.

Kevin, CEO of a large real estate brokerage firm in California had strong opinions about how ethical business should be conducted. Yet he felt that some of his brokers were cutting corners and damaging the company's reputation for the sake of short-term personal commissions. Although the outcome was positive in terms of short-term company revenues, he felt that a consistent breach of values among his employees would come back to haunt him, negatively impacting client satisfaction and long-term overall profitability.

Kevin took the courageous step of outlining the company's values and evaluating each employee (especially the high-paid, high-powered brokers) against these values through 360 evaluations. It came as no surprise to him that some of his best producers were some of the most guilty.

He showed even greater courage by meeting individually with each of the three brokers who had received the lowest-values scores, not to call them OBTs, but rather to inform them that they would need to improve their values scores within a certain period of time in order to maintain employment with the firm.

Feeling shocked and mistreated, one broker quit the next day amidst a great deal of drama. Another stayed for 30 days until she found another job with a local competitor. Kevin had prepared himself for this possibility and had determined to accept these outcomes.

However, one of the brokers genuinely tried to change, asking his team what he must do to improve in more effectively demonstrating the company's values. Sensing his sincerity, the team rallied around him, supporting his attempts to change and calling him on it when he fell back to old behaviors. He stayed with the firm and maintained his top producer status but did it in a way that didn't undermine the rest of the team and which allowed the company to build long lasting relationships with their clients.

I'll bet that you can remember a time when an OBT left your organization. Morale went up, employees danced in the aisles, productivity improved and overall results soared. It takes courage to suffer the short-term hit that can result from addressing these employees honestly and directly. However, if like Kevin you have this courage, you will have a healthier culture and more productive employees.

Consider rostering your employees on these A-B-C quadrants. Know who your players really are. Spend your time with the A and B players. The incremental improvements in their performance will yield significant results for your organization. Use the *MIH* process outlined above to coach your B-players to become A-players. Let the C's and OBTs know what they must do to avoid "job in jeopardy" status and make a commitment to manage them up or out. Don't get caught spending all your time with people who rarely make meaningful contributions to the team's overall success, and by all means, use the steps I will outline in Chapter 6 to ensure that you don't hire them in the first place.

Now that we've reviewed the process of holding people accountable that helped Rick and Kevin achieve improved success, let's look at the *personal style of coaching* required to be a courageous and effective leader who consistently holds your team accountable.

An Easy Seven-Step Formula for Personal Coaching That Works

Whether it is performance results or demonstration of values, you will need to at some point – even with the *MIH* accountability process – coach your employees. Yes, it will take a direct one-to-one conversation between you and a real person. You can't avoid it, so let's make it painless and effective by following these seven steps:

1. *Prepare yourself.* Know your "bumper sticker" and think through what you want this person to be able to say or own after a successful coaching session. For example, if you were a wildly successful coach, you might get them to say "I must be a better listener," OR "I must learn to be a great time manager," OR "I must increase my sales results." Once you know your *coaching bumper sticker*, you can "reverse engineer" your line of questions. If the person actually says this pre-prepared line at the end of the session, you will know you have been a good coach!

2. *Prepare the person you are coaching.* Ask for permission to give him or her feedback. People will always reply with a "yes," but it buys them a little time to prepare and prevents them from being blindsided.

   Create a safe environment. Start with the positives. Be specific and genuine. There are always more strengths than weaknesses in any human, so explain in some detail what you have noticed about that person's talents and contributions. (Remember, this requires you to have been a keen observer of your people.) Reviewing strengths first will relax the one being coached, because although they know that the other side is coming the "coachee" will feel that you sincerely appreciate him or her despite their shortcomings.

   In the end, your focus on and effective deployment of their strengths will serve you better than any time you spend on their weaknesses. However, the truth is that their weaknesses can derail their career, and you have an obligation to make them aware of and help them through these opportunities for improvement.

3. *Deliver the message.* Describe what they can do to be even more effective and explain why change is important. Actually use the line, "You could be even more effective if..." This line implies that they are *already* effective, but that they could and should take their success to the next level.

    Be specific rather than general. Be descriptive as opposed to evaluative. Don't tell them they are wrong, sloppy, inconsiderate and incompetent, or that you don't like the way they do things. Give concrete facts and examples (again, requiring keen observation of your people). Tie the behavior that must change to actual metrics, results and real-life situations. Don't focus on the behavior itself. Rather, explain the negative *impact* of the behavior on the team's success, the person's individual success and the individual's future with the company.

    Watch your tone and body language. If you *feel* angry, buy yourself a little time and wait to speak to the individual until you know that you will not display negative emotion. Anger does not land well and only creates defensiveness. Come from a place of genuine but firm support.

4. *Ask for replay.* Test for understanding. Ask them to paraphrase: Can they explain with sincerity what must change and why it is important to take action?

5. *Agree on a clear goal.* The wording here is important. Can they state your original bumper sticker? (i.e., "I must increase my sales to a minimum $10,000 per month.") Is there any equivocation in the way they state the goal? (i.e., "I must increase my sales to a minimum $10,000 per month, but only if Tom finally does *his* job!") Stay on this step until you know that they buy in and that achievement of the goal as they state it will resolve the issue.

6. *Create a contract.* Ask the employees to outline focused next steps – do these steps achieve the agreed-upon goal? Ask them how you should handle it if for some reason they fail to follow through. How would they want you

to follow up specifically? What do they think the repercussions should be? This allows *them* to determine the penalty of complacency, procrastination and avoidance, and they are usually harder on themselves than you would be. (You parents know that this "self imposed penalty process" also works great with kids.)

7. ***Follow through.*** For crucial coaching sessions requiring immediate change, ask the employees to summarize in a follow-up email *in their own words* an outline of their goals, their commitments and *specific* next steps with due dates. This step is important in order for them to truly own the outcome and for you to be able to detect "buyer's remorse" after they go home and digest the conversation (which you'll be able to hear in the tone of their summaries). It also represents excellent documentation in the unlikely event that progressive disciplinary action turns out to be necessary.

Having the courage to coach your team to improved performance should not be an obligation but rather a privilege that delivers extraordinary personal and professional returns. Use the seven-step *MIH* accountability process and the seven-step personal coaching approach outlined above to consistently hold people accountable without emotion, angst or hard feelings while helping them to realize their fullest potential and significantly improve your results.

Summary and Action Steps:

1. Insist on a few measurable success metrics for each team member that represent their best contributions in alignment with the company's goals and with each other's.
2. Implement a simple, fair, objective and documented process of accountability throughout your organization.
3. Have the courage and discipline to see that process through – every single month – with no exceptions.
4. Let the process be the accountability "bad guy." Use the team to ensure that every member is under the same scrutiny to deliver on their promises.
5. Roster you're A-, B- and C-players and your OBTs. Have a plan for moving them all toward A-player status.
6. Get comfortable with the truth that you must sometimes confront people

directly about their performance, and use the seven-step coaching formula to do it effectively and without emotion.

Accountability – the Bumper Sticker: Leaders have the courage to repair or replace!

6

Secret 5 – Packing Your Team with Talent

How to recruit, hire, develop and retain for competitive advantage

"Our people are our greatest asset." You hear this statement all the time. Do you believe it? Do you say the same about your team? Do you act on it? Do you truly put your team's talents to work for your company?

Most companies haul out this statement frequently and claim that it is true, but give very little systematic or regular attention to employee morale, opinions and suggestions. Oh, they have the occasional picnic, holiday party or other "team building" event, but rarely do they mine the gold of employee opinions and suggestions. They prefer to hire expensive consultants who interview employees and whose input they consolidate into a lengthy, colorful and expensive report of recommendations that are rarely implemented. They could save themselves time and expense by simply and literally valuing their employee base.

Your employees are the people closest to your customers – the ones who build the relationships that grow your business and the ones who actually deliver your products and services. Do you want to know what your customers are thinking? Ask the closest source. They happen to be on your payroll!

The painful truth is that we are only as effective as the people we draw to us. This chapter will show you how companies that recruit, develop and retain the greatest talent and then deploy that talent effectively, win. Not the companies with the greatest strategic plans or accountability systems. Not the companies with the smartest or most charismatic leaders. The clear winners are those companies that attract and retain the best talent and then listen to their employees' ideas. The clear losers are those companies that continue to make the top five recruiting mistakes...

The Top Five Recruiting Mistakes

You've certainly heard of a misfire, but have you ever had a "mis-hire"? The effects of both can be similar, metaphorically speaking. Thinking back on one of your mis-hires... how soon did you know it occurred? If you are honest with yourself, you'll realize that it was within days or weeks, sometimes hours from the time the new recruit walked through the door. There are professional interviewees out there who can earn the job offer, but then seem to bear no resemblance to the person who walks through the door on the first day at the new job.

We may recognize a mis-hire quickly, yet how long do we keep that mis-hire around? The national corporate average is three years! How do you explain the fact that we know within weeks we've made a mistake, yet retain them for so long? If you search your soul, you'll know that answer. Our credibility is at stake for hiring them in the first place. We think we can "fix" them. We think we'll rub off on them. We don't want to go through the painful process of firing and re-hiring. We *hope* they'll get better – heck, we've invested a lot time and effort into them already!

What is the cost of a mis-hire? If you accumulate the costs of recruiting, interviewing, signing bonuses, actual compensation, training, benefits, overhead, lack of productivity, mistakes, missed opportunities, severance and potential lawsuits over an average three-year period, the cost is staggering. We can no longer afford to hire in a cavalier fashion and just hope it works out – this approach is just too painful and expensive.

Why do we hire so badly?

1. ***We're lazy.*** We don't do our homework. We think we know what we're looking for and that we'll know it when we see it. I have interviewed several

recruiters for the exact same position in a given company, asking about their criteria for the perfect candidate. The conflicting range of responses I receive from them is scary. Until you know clearly what you are looking for, why you are looking for it, and everyone involved in the recruiting process agrees with you, you are doomed to be worked over by those professional interviewees mentioned above.

Want to remedy this problem quickly and easily? Consider completing a simple job description such as this one below. (This is in addition to the seven-page legal form that requires the candidate to be able to sit for a certain length of time or to perform his or her "duties as assigned.")

Job Description

NAME:	Position Title:
Manager Name:	

The Top 5 Essential Duties or Key Responsibilities of this Position:
1.
2.
3.
4.
5.

The Minimum Experience Required of this Position:
1.
2.
3.
4.
5.

The Top 5 Job Competencies required for success in this position (choose from 50 outlined attached)
1.
2.
3.
4.
5.

The Top 5 Success Metrics (How we will measure success):
1.
2.
3.
4.
5.

dsamih
Consulting LLC *Define Success And Make It Happen*

The thought process required to complete this one-page form should be conducted prior to interviewing so you can know exactly what you are looking for in a potential candidate.

This exercise also helps you to prepare an answer for the question that every qualified candidate should ask of the company looking to hire him or her: "If I'm wildly successful, how will you know? What will you see in a year?" I advise candidates always to ask and never to accept a position when that question can't be answered, because without knowing the answer, how could anyone possibly achieve success? Do you want to attract successful people to your organization? Be clear with them about what success will look like.

A large national benefits and payroll company that was known for attracting top talent found itself over the course of two years experiencing 40% turnover! Charlotte, the regional VP, was appalled to discover such a costly statistic and asked me to come in to help them analyze the problem. I met with seven hiring managers in the department experiencing the highest turnover, and had expected to find inexperienced leaders who were rough around the edges when it came to interpersonal skills. On the contrary, I discovered that these folks were committed, concerned, intelligent and insightful about what employees needed and wanted.

I asked about the recruiting process and learned that Human Resources was screening the applicants and that the hiring managers were disappointed with the caliber and consistency of the candidates referred. Further, they found that enthusiastic new recruits became very quickly sullen, introverted and frustrated.

I asked about the criteria for a successful candidate, per the one-page job description, and found that the seven hiring managers had seven very different points of view about what was required in a successful recruit. No wonder Human Resources had been ineffective. It turns out that because all the screeners and interviewers were unclear about what success looked like, it became very unclear to the new recruits as well. In fact, many had actually hired on thinking that their role was in customer service when they were actually being hired for sales positions! No surprise that their enthusiasm quickly turned to dismay.

We spent an afternoon reaching agreement about each section of the above job description, using the considerable combined experience of these hiring managers. We built a recruitment and interview guideline that both HR and all interviewers could follow. The result? Because everyone involved in the interview process knew exactly what they were looking for and how to find it, turnover among new recruits dropped from 40% to 5% in just one year.

This job description is so important that I suggest reviewing it with your well-qualified candidates during the interview process so they can fully understand your expectations and also realize that accountability is built into those expectations. I even have my candidates sign the document as an implicit contract of understanding before they begin their first day.

2. **We're desperate.** We don't like to interview. We consider the hiring process a distraction from our job, a pain in the neck and something HR should actually do for us. We should just be able to have the right people show up and then manage them well. Given this bias, we tell ourselves that the next candidate who walks through the door is the right person for the position, and we hold onto that belief until the candidate says something to screw it up. They are basically in until they prove themselves out. Given the cost of a mis-hire as outlined above, we need to look at this entirely in the reverse. A candidate should be basically *out* until he or she proves him/herself *in*.

3. **We talk too much.** The best way to keep the candidate from saying something to screw it up is to not let them talk. Instead, we talk about the position, the company, ourselves and our history, but rarely get the candidate to talk (or even give him or her an *opportunity* to talk).

Throughout my career, I have made it a point to go on every interview someone asked me to consider. Never turn down an opportunity until you know what it is! This decision allowed me to get inside the heads of industry leaders early in my career and to learn from some of the best.

Although, one of my most memorable interviews stands out as typical of a dysfunctional interview style. It was with the CEO of a healthcare company who was considering me for his VP of Operations position. He was a very nice man who went to great pains to welcome me, shake my hand and learn my name, after which I said nothing for the rest of the interview. He explained how he had come to join the company, the challenges he had faced, the importance of this operations position and why he needed to ensure that he hired the best talent. He talked for more than 45 minutes while I smiled and nodded. He then declared with great enthusiasm that I was clearly his best candidate so far! How the heck would he know?

It is important to have a thorough, prepared, structured interview guide that queries each candidate on the same open-ended questions in the same way for each interview. This was part of the recruitment guideline we built for the benefits and payroll company, resulting in the 85% drop in turnover.

4. *We're naive.* When we do ask questions, we invite yes or no answers or prompt the candidate for the correct answer: "Do you have integrity? Are you a hard worker?" Rather, we should ask open-ended questions that cause the interviewee to reflect on his or her career and to actually explain how they have demonstrated in the past the quality for which you are looking. For example, "Explain a time when your integrity was truly tested. What happened and how did you handle it?" Or, "Describe a time when you had to work harder than you ever have before. What was the situation, how did you feel about it and what was the result?"

5. *We're impatient.* We try to fill the position in one interview, failing to use a panel with differing perspectives and failing to see the candidate in different situations over time. Teach a panel of managers and peers what to look for, given the simple job description above, and how to interview both effectively and legally. Grade all responses on the same criteria per the above recruitment guideline, and compare scores for each candidate when the interviews are complete. Peers who perform the actual job for which the candidate is being considered will often have insights that the manager can't have and, once part of the hiring process, will work diligently to assist the candidate they helped to select to be more successful in that job.

There is no question that what I outline here requires an investment of time. But think about the colossal waste of time and money spent on a mis-hire. Make the selection process for your organization a rite of passage and a job offer a privilege for which the new hire feels honored. Let candidates know that you are careful about who joins your team and that because of this intensive interview process you are highly confident that once hired, they will be successful and valued contributors. Like other clients who have used this process, you will consistently attract A-players and ensure their success on the team.

Now, how do you hold on to those A-players?

The Top 10 Employee-Retention Mistakes

Why do some organizations experience such high turnover, which is even worse when it is among their best performers?

1. *We don't have our act together.* On-boarding is the process of ensuring that new recruits have everything they need, when the need it, so they can be productive quickly and optimize your investment in them. We have one chance to create a positive new employee experience.

   We should make them feel welcomed and valued, giving them prior to arrival and electronically all the paperwork they'll need to complete so they can do it online at their own convenience. Give them company policies, an employee handbook and benefit information in a clear, succinct user-friendly way. Give them an updated organization chart and a space/desk/people map. Don't make them learn the hard way and through tribal knowledge how to best maneuver the company.

   And for the love of Pete, have their space, their phone and computer installed and ready for them prior to arrival. Don't make them beg for resources and a place to work. Flowers or a welcome sign in the space is a nice touch and so is a welcome letter or video from the CEO and/or the manager. Okay, you may be saying to yourself, flowers and a welcome sign? Some of your organizations are small and you don't have the resources to provide the small touches. But you get the idea. You can still go out of your way to make the new recruit feel welcome and at home.

   Challenge new recruits with a training calendar, a list of topics they must learn in order to be proficient in their jobs and a list of people from whom they might learn those topics. Then hold *the new recruit* responsible to complete his or her training against that list.

   The manager should set expectations and work with new recruits on success metrics that represent their most important contributions. Be sure they know what their success metric goal targets are for the first month, the first six months, the first year and so on.

Assign a mentor or buddy to help them navigate through their first few weeks. Making the first few weeks productive and welcoming for new recruits will go a long way in securing their longevity.

2. ***We don't coach.*** Or we don't know how, but the processes outlined in the last chapter should make that easy. Use the monthly *MIH (Make It Happen)* meeting process to consistently provide feedback, best practice ideas and suggestions for overcoming obstacles.

Use the seven-step formula for personal coaching to give them ongoing and meaningful feedback, seeing it as an opportunity to take new employees' contributions to the next level rather than as an obligation to be confrontational.

When coaching, focus most of your time on your best players. Wait... that doesn't sound right? We think that the best performers don't need as much coaching as the poor performers? Think again. We often focus most of our time on the worst performers, the drama-creators and the difficult employees who very rarely become top talent, thereby ignoring our best players.

The incremental improvements made in your best players through effective coaching far outweighs the improvements you'll find by working with your least successful players. Focus your time on the 20% who achieve 80% of the results. Be succinct and clear with the lowest performers and OBTs regarding specifically what *they* must do to raise their own level of performance and to earn your time.

3. ***We focus on weaknesses instead of strengths.*** Although employee weaknesses can derail careers and we need to be honest with them about those weaknesses, we garner much more productivity by focusing on strengths. We also need to understand that people's weaknesses are usually their strengths wielded a little too heavily. For example, Tom can be decisive – a nice strength. Wielded too heavily? He doesn't listen. Heather is an employee advocate – a great strength. Wielded too heavily? She makes excuses for people and doesn't hold them accountable.

Every leadership strength if used in excess becomes a weakness. Our goal in reviewing derailing weaknesses with employees is not for them to attempt a

180-degree turn in the opposite direction, because in doing so we lose their strengths. What we want is to get the employee to pull back the pendulum a little so they don't use that same tool all the time. Have you ever heard the line that when you're a hammer, everything looks to you like a nail? Well, we want our best talent to be a little more agile than that.

According to a 2006 Gallup study, we achieve 80% actively engaged employees when we focus on their strengths, 44% actively engaged employees when we focus on their weaknesses and only 4% actively engaged employees when we ignore them.

Why are so many employees less engaged when they are ignored? Negative attention is preferable to no attention. You might think that this statement only applies to children who are ignored by parents, but employees feel the same when they are ignored by their managers. Ignored employees will act out their unhappiness seeking some attention. Every day, these workers can undermine what their engaged co-workers accomplish.

Remember when we talked about how any given human's strengths far outweigh their weaknesses? Look for the best in your team and deploy them according to those strengths. They will walk through fire for you.

4. *We don't have time for no stinking performance reviews!* It is imperative with both new hires and existing staff to assess their performance against results, required competencies and company values. Evaluate where they are and give them honest feedback. Don't use performance review forms that involve flowery descriptions of their activities and good intentions. Focus on results. Use the outline given in the last chapter for establishing effective, meaningful and proactive performance reviews.

    As input to the review process, consider conducting the 360 evaluation at performance review time, allowing you to include the input of the manager, peers and direct reports. Make the survey easy to complete, and ensure that it is forwarded to those most affected by the performance of the employee. You might use easy online survey tools like Survey Monkey or Zoomerang to make the process both painless and anonymous.

    Why go to all this 360 trouble? Because people often manage up, out and down differently, and each component of the circle may have a different point of view. Offering the employee well-developed, anonymous and recurring-theme feedback often prevents denial and allows the employee to focus clearly on real-life issues that can be improved without the damaging focus on "who said what."

Rather than a time-consuming obligation that is usually avoided or procrastinated, you can use a meaningful performance review process to coach, grow your bench strength and create loyalty.

5. *We can't answer "what's next?"* We don't outline for employees what kind of career growth they might expect through succession planning, career-pathing and mentorship programs.

Succession planning is about looking down on the organization from the top leader's point of view, determining who the key lieutenants are who would create the largest hole in the organization should something happen to them. The leaders then determine who the best internal candidates are for filling those positions. A skill/experience-gap analysis is conducted to identify the delta between the veterans and the candidates, putting in place specific, scheduled internal and external training programs to fill those gaps for the rising stars.

Career-pathing is from the perspective of the employee rather than the leader. Where could I go next? What is the natural progression of employees' careers if they stay with this organization? How have others before them advanced their learning and experience here? Be prepared to answer these questions with well-documented facts and you will keep your best talent. Succession plans and career-path programs should inform and enhance one another.

Finally, mentorship programs allow promising rising stars to be paired with more veteran players who cannot only coach them to better performance but can accelerate their growth by helping them to avoid the pitfalls of first-time management responsibility. The two main criteria for good mentors? They must be willing and able to tell you the brutal truth, and they must have your best interest at heart. Find people in your organization who meet these simple criteria and pair them with your rising stars. Both will benefit! But be sure to explain that ownership of this relationship belongs to the one being mentored. The mentee should preserve the mentor's time, own the lessons to be learned, do the homework and follow up as assigned.

Build a succession plan, involve your employees in career-pathing and implement a mentorship program in your organization and you will create a much larger percentage of actively engaged employees while significantly reducing the turnover of your best talent.

6. *We guess wrong.* We assume that we know how employees would like to be rewarded when successful. They want the same things we do, right? Wrong.

While running a division of a large healthcare company, I was guilty of thinking I knew what employees wanted. Everyone wants recognition, right? So I made a big point of holding quarterly employee celebrations for those who had exceeded their success metrics, giving them ostentatious presentations of awards, gift certificates and verbal tributes before a large assembly of employees, friends and family members. Some of those poor people were so embarrassed that you could feel them wanting to sink through the floor.

Employee motives run the gamut from money to time off to policy input to control over workload assignments or scheduling. The list is endless. Don't guess. *Ask* how employees would like to be celebrated when successful. Very often, they just want more control over their lives. Give them whatever control you can.

By the way, do you know what kind of jobs are the most stressful? Is it those of Presidents? Nurses? Kings? Teachers? Wall Street tycoons? Waitresses? CEOs? Supervisors? Actually, the highest-stress jobs are those with high volume and limited control, so nurses, teachers, waitresses and supervisors have the toughest jobs. I learned this the day I first became president of my company. Quite unexpectedly, my stress dropped dramatically. It's good to be queen! Acknowledge the folks who have less autonomy and control of time with all you can offer them in terms of input, flexibility and work/life balance.

Most important, reward their successes frequently with myriad no-cost options that *they* really care about.

7. *We're chicken.* We know there are poor performers, bullies and prima donnas on our team, but we fail to take action, hoping they will get better over time so we won't have to have a difficult confrontation. The message we send to the rest of the team? Results, competencies, values and culture don't really count. Why should your best talent stay and try harder when underperformers and bullies aren't held to task and the remaining employees have to pick up the slack?

   We must have the courage to follow a consistent coaching process and to ensure repercussions for those who don't live up to their commitments. I recommend a three-strikes rule. Once you have coached an employee three times on an important behavioral change to which the employee has committed, (using the seven-step coaching formula) and he or she still fails to follow through, use the organization's progressive disciplinary process to free up his or her future!

8. *We don't stop to smell the roses.* We don't take time to offer recognition or praise for work well done. I don't mean parties, picnics, expensive gifts or formal occasions. What talented employees want most from you is sincere and *specific* praise. Which of the following three accolades would *you* rather hear?

   "Tom, great job with that client!" OR, "Tom, you make me proud." OR, "Tom, I was amazed at how you handled that frustrated client the other day. You were calm and you calmed the client. You listened to his concerns and gave him confidence that the problem would be fixed. You were like a client whisperer! I wish we had 10 people with your skill in client management." Of course, you'd prefer the last one, especially if your name is Tom!

   People crave this kind of praise detail. Observe them so you can give it to them – publicly if you can. You can very quickly build the kind of energy and enthusiasm that launches a team to the next level of success.

   Finally, I have found no more powerful tool of recognition than a simple hand-written note or voicemail that gives people specific, genuine feedback on something I've caught people *doing* right. It costs nothing but can be remembered and treasured for a lifetime. Have you ever saved a wonderful note that someone wrote to you because it stated with emotion the positive impact you'd had on the individual? Even a Post-It™ note or a voicemail delivered while you are driving home will do in a pinch and can impact your employee's sense of pride and motivation more than you'll ever know. You'll get some idea of its impact when you see your note posted on their cubicle walls for years, even after they've move to a new cubicle.

9. *We don't listen.* We hire expensive consultants to tell us what our employees think. When our employees try to tell us themselves, we ignore or discount them, or we label them as troublemakers. Our biggest single asset is our employee base, and we don't mine the gold.

The best leaders listen intently – both formally and informally. They invite employees to drop in – not to undermine those managers beneath them by listening to complaints they haven't shared with their manager. Rather, they have an open-door policy to welcome new ideas. They take employees to lunch – not just their favorites but those with whom they have little contact. They wander the office routinely, collecting gems of ideas and insights from those closest to the customer. They conduct formal surveys for both employee satisfaction and ideas for improving the organization. Then they report the results of those surveys back to the employees and outline specific action steps to be taken.

When employees feel listened to and that their ideas are valued, they want to go the extra mile for you and your organization.

10. *We're jerks!* The number-one reason any employee leaves an organization? His or her boss. From Norman Drummond, a motivational speaker:

> **More than 70% of people leave their jobs because of the way they are led.**

It is the relationship with an employee's immediate manager that will determine how long he or she will stay as well as that employee's level of productivity. If employees feel that their manager doesn't care about them as people or that the manager will always choose the company's best interest over theirs, they begin to look for other opportunities. Even worse, if the manager has those derailing qualities of condescending arrogance, credit-grabbing pride, self-serving intimidation, and a whole host of others that stem from insecurity and fear, you can fully expect to chalk off your talent.

If you have a manager who is able to avoid the first nine mistakes above but is guilty of this tenth mistake you will still lose your best players. Such managers may try to convince themselves that the employee's leaving had nothing to do with them... that the employee was seduced by a job closer to home or by one offering more money. However, you'll know in your heart that it was *the manager*. Evaluate your managers with short but effective employee surveys. Take a look at who on your team creates loyalty and who has frequent and costly turnover. Through assessment and coaching, you can ensure a culture of caring managers who create both loyalty and employee retention.

Many leaders have decided that the most important thing they can do to enhance their careers is to surround themselves with talent. In doing so, they consistently find that life is easier, they don't have to work as hard, amazing things are accomplished, work is simply more fun and they are advanced in the organization! I'm sure this will be an easy decision for *you* too.

Summary and Action Steps:

1. Convince yourself, if you haven't already, that your people truly are your greatest asset.
2. Put specific plans in place, with accountable parties and due dates, to treat your people as such.
3. Look closely at your recruiting process across the board. With this process are you likely to be a magnet for great talent?
4. Is your turnover higher than you'd like it to be? Look inward at your team. Using the above 10 retention keys, determine what you can do specifically to create a healthier environment for A-players to thrive.
5. Pay attention to the managers in your organization who attract, develop and retain promotable talent. What are they doing right?

Staffing – the Bumper Sticker: Create an environment that is a magnet for talent – it will be your greatest competitive advantage.

7

Secret 6 - Creating Communication Magic

Your single most important leadership edge

Developing strong communication skills is *the* single most important device in your corporate tool kit and the greatest influencing factor in promotability. Have you ever known someone who had extremely smooth verbal and written communication skills yet almost no other redeeming qualities? What happens to them in the organization? You watch as they are promoted! So what would happen if you added these skills to your considerable list of strengths? Perhaps this is the key to *your* next promotion.

Communication skills cover a broad spectrum of techniques and talents outlined in this chapter. In this series of easy steps you will learn to handle each of the following difficult aspects of becoming a powerful communicator:

- Ensuring that you are truly heard
- Creating healthy debate
- Communicating skillfully with your boss
- Managing successful meetings
- Avoiding the five biggest obstacles to effective communication
- Building emotional intelligence

By following these steps, you will learn *what* to communicate, *how* to communicate in the most compelling way, and how to ensure that your message is truly heard. When it comes to communication tools, some of my clients tell me that they are asking for a drink of water and I shoot them with a fire hose! Focus only those specific tools that will help you to improve *your* communication skills. Now let's get started…

Err On the Side of Too Much Info!

Communication is almost every company's biggest weakness. I have surveyed hundreds of companies on their strengths and weaknesses, and some aspect of communication consistently comes out as their number-one area for improvement. Employees complain about the lack of effective organizational communication because they want to be *in the know*. They need to know the bigger picture so they can make informed decisions. Once they believe that they are in the know they feel more important and secure.

Upon reviewing these employee survey results, senior executives are often exasperated to learn that their considerable attempts at communication have fallen short.

John, a well-meaning but frustrated CEO once said to me, "I told these guys my vision during our all-company meeting last year! What do you mean they don't understand our vision?" I had to remind John that you must tell an employee about an idea or concept at least *five* times before it registers and they believe that you mean for them to take it seriously. Five times! Why? Because they have heard from their leaders so many "flavors of the month" and they hope that if they just keep their heads down and continue their work that this "new direction" will fizzle like all the others.

So how do you decide what to tell them, how much and how often? Offer more information rather than less. Do you want people to think and act as you would? Tell them what you know – often and effectively! Here's an example.

I was once consulting with Jim and Marie, a brother-and-sister team, under whose leadership a small industrial equipment company had grown to a $60 million concern. The company had grown to a size where Jim and Marie could no longer manage the business effectively themselves, so they hired four of their grown children to manage the key divisions. However, they felt uncomfortable about sharing too much information with their offspring. They explained to me that they gave information to all their staff only on a "need-to-know basis."

Translation: "We don't trust our people (not even our children) and they aren't important enough to know what we know."

Yet every month, they lamented their children's lack of business acumen because they had consistently failed to make appropriate cost-benefit decisions. The end result? Profits were waning. I asked Jim and Marie if their kids had been given profit/loss information regarding their various divisions and if they had negotiated specific goals for improving them, to which both brother and sister simultaneously shouted, "Of course not! If they knew how well we were doing, they would expect a bigger piece of the pie!"

Hmmm.... How can we ask our lieutenants to be smarter about managing the business if we don't allow them access to specific information that would help them do their jobs better? Information, measurable results, process improvements and data analysis are key to successful growth companies.

Once Jim and Marie agreed to negotiate with their managers clear success metrics for their divisions and then give them timely and accurate profit and loss information so they could report status on those metrics, profits climbed.

Give employees the bigger picture so they can make good decisions. And when you communicate this big picture, focus less on the *how* and more on the *what and why*.

Let me explain:

Many of us deliver information in terms of how we want our people to move forward, without ever telling them what success looks like and why it is important. We have done the job thousands of times ourselves and can tell them exactly *how* to proceed, but we rarely dedicate the time required to think through what success looks like or the impact of achieving that success so that we can articulate *that* well. Empower your teams with the information that allows them to think rather than to follow orders. It seems that many managers insist on explaining to those they perceive as "important," the *what and why* of their vision; to "unimportant people" they explain the *how*. People can actually determine how we feel about them by which approach we use.

Give your teams the bigger-picture information they need to be empowered and successful. Tell them often. Give them the framework that helps them to think like you do so they can make the choices you would.

Manage the Grapevine

Leaders often tell me that they have a difficult communication to deliver regarding lay-offs, compensation changes, etc. and that they are working to make sure every detail is clear before communicating the bad news. Sound reasonable? *Big* mistake!

I mentioned previously that people want to be in the know. This is particularly true in stressful situations. If they don't hear the news from their leaders, they will fill in the information gap, listening to the grapevine and speculating possibilities with their coworkers. The information they "fill in" is almost *always* uglier and scarier than the truth. You can avoid this problem by following the classic rule of public relations:

> ## Tell good news fast; tell bad news faster!

Manage the message. Earn the team's trust that they will always hear the latest scoop, honestly and directly, from you. What if you don't have all the answers? That's okay. Tell them what you know when you know it. Tell them what you don't know and when you might know the information they seek.

Avoid offering a continuously positive spin on tough communications. Don't get me wrong... there is always opportunity in adversity and you should be clear about that. But people can smell propaganda a mile away and they will perceive a spin doctor as disingenuous, deceptive and manipulative. Be authentic – let people know both the good and bad news; outline the realistic possibilities.

In lay-offs, mergers or other scary situations for employees, err on the side of over-communicating. In fact, simply letting them know that you don't have any new information is comforting to those worried for their futures. Here's an example...

I was once responsible for the operational merger of two healthcare companies. The tension regarding job consolidations and lay-offs was palpable. I realized just how high emotions were running one morning as I walked into the office and said "hi" to a group of employees talking in the foyer. As I walked past, I overheard one individual in the group say, "What do you think she meant by that?!"

Knowledge, no matter how painful, is less painful than fear of the unknown. Listen to what worries the team and make it a priority to communicate clearly and often on those topics. For long-term stress situations, such as a merger, consider weekly newsletters or 15-minute conference calls, updating the team on progress and discussing openly the most controversial issues, offering the facts as you know them. Welcome questions and answer as honestly as you can.

Courageous communication is not about having all the facts – facts often take time to develop. It is about knowing and facing your team's fears with honesty and empathy at the earliest possible time *without* having all the facts. Leaders who do this consistently are consistently trusted.

Successful Waterfall Communication

Great! You have decided to deliver more meaningful, big-picture information to your teams, but notice that it doesn't seem to reach the lower levels of the organization, or that it becomes garbled once it gets there. Want a formula for ensuring powerful communication throughout the organization every time?

Imagine a waterfall in your mind. I'm guessing you can see how it relates to communication in your office. Here is how it works:

No matter what position you hold on the "org chart," at the end of any *important* meeting *you* lead, determine the five top "bumper stickers" that resulted from that meeting. What were the key decisions, outcomes or directions? Leaders, please don't summarize the key issues yourself; rather, ask the team what *they* think the top five are. This is a great way to end any meeting. It helps you to know if the team understands and agrees on the most important outcomes. Get these outcomes to "bumper stickers" and put them in writing so there is no room for interpretation. This exercise will either quickly align the team or surface disconnects that can be quickly resolved.

Decide which, if any, of these top five bumper stickers should not be communicated to the rest of the organization for some reason. Sanitize confidential information if you must, but as we reviewed before, have really good reasons for labeling something "confidential" – not much truly is.

Tell your lieutenants that you expect *all staff* to know about these top business bumper stickers by end of week.

Conduct at least weekly MBWAs in your office (Management By Walking Around) and ask the people at the lowest level of the organization what they know about the top bumper stickers. If they are clueless, there is a gap in your waterfall communication!

Hold your lieutenants accountable for any disconnects or gaps in communication. If they know you will follow up with "frontline MBWAs," they will ferret out the offenders and make effective Waterfall Communication happen consistently, especially if *they* are the offenders.

This easy process ensures that your team is motivated to cascade quality communication throughout the organization, while avoiding the trap of miscommunication, like that which occurs in the children's game of *telephone*.

The Five-Step Process for Healthy Debate

Did you know that 20% of all leaders display "emperor with no clothes-like" behavior and that 40% aren't aware that their employees frequently roll their eyes about them behind their backs? You can easily avoid being one of these statistics. I'll show you how below, but first, a story…

I once had a client whose culture allowed the senior team to debate within an inch of its life every decision. If someone didn't get his or her way, they were permitted to revisit the issue and continue the debate at all subsequent meetings until they did get their way. I had another client whose hierarchical leader was so intimidating that no decisions were debated or questioned for fear of retribution, so meetings involved a lot of head nodding and one-way communication. Which client practiced healthy debate?

The answer is neither.

What follows is a five-step formula for creating healthy debate that works every time to build an atmosphere of absolute trust, while securing the best, most informed decisions:

1. Tell your team that they have permission to state any ugly truth as they know it. They should assume that there are no sacred cows. (I haven't found an organization yet that doesn't have one – do you know yours?) There should be nothing that can't be challenged. Encourage politically incorrect points of view. Make a conscious decision not to be the emperor with no clothes!

2. Explain that the initiator of the ugly truth must present at least one potential recommendation or solution. No grenades allowed.

3. The initiator must then state his/her most compelling reasons as to why the proposed recommendations or solutions should be adopted.

4. The team should then discuss opposing points of view, debating the pros and cons of the proposed solution, and then the leader should make a decision.

5. Win or lose, the initiator of the idea *must get on the bus* with that decision!

Do not allow decisions that have been effectively debated to be revisited, unless there is *new* information. Revisits are time wasters that allow one person's ego to get in the way of productive meetings and forward momentum.

Using this five-step process consistently, both of the clients I mentioned built healthy cultures of candid debate without suffering either "yes men" or unproductive ongoing conflict. Further, both teams were much happier and got a lot more done.

The Secret for Managing Up and Out as Well as Down

Which is your primary job function? Managing your boss, your peers or your direct reports? Ninety percent of all leaders I've interviewed say that their top priority is to manage their direct reports. Why? Because that's where they feel the greatest sense of control. Yet when your boss and peers are not aligned how effective can you be?

I once coached Mark, a very bright but struggling manufacturing executive who harbored unfortunate authority issues, saying about his boss, Steve:

- Well, if he's qualified to be my boss he shouldn't have to be managed.
- Steve should know what's going on, and if he can't figure it out that's his problem.
- My team's results should speak for themselves.

I asked Mark how well this strategy was working for him. He had to admit that he felt his boss didn't appreciate him and that he felt he wasn't all that highly regarded by his peers.

An important part of your job is to assist in creating alignment, clarity and unity among your peers and your manager. What follows is a system I shared with Mark for achieving this with a minimum of effort:

Send an email every Friday to your manager, peers and direct reports with no more than nine bullet-point bumper stickers:

- The first one to three bullets outline your team's top successes for the week. For those of you who have trouble with self-promotion, this will help you – your manager can't possibly know all your best wins unless you tell him or her. Let others know what your team has done well – it invites powerful praise for your team. Plus, 52 weeks of such documentation can be invaluable at your next performance review. As a side benefit, your direct reports will work hard to be mentioned in those first bullet points – an inexpensive but powerful motivator!

- The next one to three bullets outline your team's top *challenges* for the week. Why share the dirty laundry? Because it allows you to be transparent about the tough issues you face. No secrets. No surprises. This lets your manager and your team members know that you are on top of the issues. Further, you just might get some ideas and support from the others and you are letting them know about your obstacles without whining about them.

- The next one to three bullets outline your team's top *priorities* for next week. The recipients will see that you are effectively managing your time and that you have the discipline to focus on what is most important. This also gives your manager and peers an opportunity to disagree with your priorities while giving your direct reports an opportunity to understand them. Your team may also tell you about a sense of urgency they have about something that is a blind spot for you.

In the body of the email, invite the recipients to provide feedback, advice and concerns. Welcome and encourage push-back and inquiry. This is your opportunity to achieve both alignment and proactive conflict resolution rather than reactive second guessing from either your manager or your peers.

If you never get a response, continue the three to nine-bullet email anyway! It is difficult at performance review time for your manager to say you have been off-track all year when you have given him or her 52 opportunities to voice an opposing point of view.

After implementing the weekly Friday e-mail, Mark was amazed at how quickly his relationship with Steve improved. Steve had felt that Mark had been evading him, and therefore, had something to hide. This had caused Steve to increase his oversight of Mark, which caused Mark to further withdraw from him.

When Mark *initiated* the weekly nine-bullet email, Steve suddenly responded with open and animated discussions about problems, solutions and available resources. Steve felt that Mark was confiding in him and Mark felt more appreciated and valued by Steve, because, in fact, he was! Mark's investment of 10 minutes a week in proactive communication with his boss, peers and subordinates resulted in a much improved performance review and a more successful team.

Following this easy nine-bullet email approach will allow *you* to enhance your team's (and yours) results and reputations in less than 10 minutes a week!

Now that you're managing up better, let's talk about getting your *bosses* to agree with your goals and objectives. We call this getting them to the yes, and there are five steps involved. (You knew there would be, right?)

Five Proven Steps to Get Your Boss to YES

Leaders are continuously barraged by their direct reports with requests for resources. These reports often sound like kids begging their parents for "stuff" (i.e., they might want training, enhanced technology or expensive policy changes). Leaders can't say yes to every request or they would quickly bankrupt the organization. The best leaders make these resource-allocation decisions based on clear cost-benefit analyses and potential for a solid return on investment (ROI), but they are often burdened with trying to figure out what that return might be when they receive only surface emotional pleas from their team. Remember the kid analogy: "We need to have X or we won't be productive. Our competitors all have X – why can't we? Morale will continue to decline if we don't get X. If we can't get X, I won't be able to achieve my goals."

Refuse this kind of request. Teach your people how to ask for resources like business owners. Teach them how to make it easy for you to say yes and to get used to hearing *no* if they fail to follow these five simple request guidelines, each of which should be answered with one simple, well thought-through sentence:

1. What do you need and why do you need it?
2. What will it cost? (Consider all costs.)
3. How will it benefit the company?
4. What is your projected return on investment?
5. By what date will you achieve that ROI?

Wouldn't you love it if your people asked for resources this way? Teach them how to do it. Get them to do their homework up front and decide not to ask if they can't offer a compelling ROI story. That said, I wouldn't require this process for decisions on holiday parties or requests for supplies, but for anything representing a major cost to your company have your team follow the discipline to ask professionally. They will grow as business leaders and your resource-allocation decisions will be a breeze.

Now that we know how to communicate resource requests, how should we communicate when dealing with chaos?

What to Do in Chaos

Have you ever been to an emotional meeting during which people talk *at* each other, no ideas are really landing, people seem to be arguing different agendas, several get frustrated, nothing gets resolved and you leave the meeting with no clear decisions or action steps? Do you suspect that you'll be revisiting the same issue at the next meeting and that you will likely experience the same unproductive result? Do you want to sound brilliant? Ask the one question for which you will never get in trouble, no matter what your position on the organization chart. Simply and quietly ask the group, *"What is the goal? Why are we here?"*

You don't even have to know the answer. People will literally quiet down, think you're brilliant, and begin asking themselves what they think the group is trying to accomplish. Go around the room and ask each participant to state their viewpoint in a short, succinct sentence as to what the goal of the meeting or problem at hand is. You will be amazed at the discrepancies.

You can waste an incredible amount of time debating the possibilities and repercussions of an issue when the members of your team aren't in agreement on what the issue is. The time spent gaining agreement on the goal, no matter how much time is required, is time well spent. If you can't get that goal to a bumper sticker (or at least a short sentence), you've left too much room for interpretation and scope creep. Any effort you put into the problem before getting agreement on the goal is time and effort wasted.

I was once called into a mortgage company by its CEO who was frustrated that his cross-functional team had spent a full year of effort and in excess of $1 million on an IT project that had literally no outcome or results to date. The project was intended to improve operational costs and productivity, but it had actually deteriorated both, leaving the team floundering, angry and discouraged. He asked me to meet with them to "fix them" and to "make them play nice in the sandbox."

I met with the 14-person team on a Tuesday morning at 8:00 a.m. and opened the meeting with this question, "What is the goal of this project?" Three hours later, the group was still arguing in an animated fashion about that goal. Is there any question why the team had failed?

How does this situation happen so often? Frankly, there is a lack of leadership and clarity from the beginning as to what the team is trying to accomplish. Scope creep is inevitable in this scenario; everyone interprets his/her individual silo needs as actually being in alignment with the original project goal.

Start today to require your team to have a succinct, well-stated goal for every project, every meeting, every voicemail and every email. Many of my clients place a small plaque on their desks reminding them to ask, "What is the goal?"

Know the answer to that question for *everything* you do. (By the way, don't allow "stream of consciousness" communications. Teach your team the refreshing economy of words that comes with having a clear bumper sticker goal for each communication and reverse engineering from there.)

There is probably no more powerful tool in this chapter on communication than that of insisting on goal clarity in all types of communications. You can take your own leadership and communication skills up a notch by simply answering almost every question or problem with this simple question, "What is the goal?"

The Five Biggest Obstacles to Effective Communication in the Office: Who is Guilty?

Picture someone in your office with whom you have difficult communications. Picturing the face? Now take a look at the following most frequent obstacles to effective communications in the office. Which ones get in the way for you and this person?

1. *Inappropriate use of time or place*

Choose a venue for tough communications that works: Let people get coffee and get settled in the morning; don't tackle them as they are walking in or out of the door. (Think about how you feel when you are jumped on without being in the proper frame of mind or appropriate space.)

Don't make public that which should be private. Praise publicly, coach privately. Don't preach to a group when the message is intended for an individual. Talk to that person privately and directly. Preaching to a group for one person's benefit looks like the behavior of a weak conflict avoider, whereas conducting individual coaching when appropriate makes you appear strong and willing to confront important issues.

Watch for people's mood and temperament. Tackle tough issues when the person you need to speak with will be most receptive, but don't use this as an excuse to avoid talking with them all together!

Go to neutral ground, such as a conference room for such discussions.

2. *Inappropriate use of email*

Follow agreed-upon and implemented rules of engagement for email (I'll provide some examples later), but never let your team use email when coaching or criticizing, for anything emotional, for complex problem resolution or anytime they would *rather* use email to avoid confrontation. This is the coward's way out.

3. *Preoccupations and distractions*

Do you know a master multi-tasker on your team? When someone asks if they have a minute, do they invite the person in but continue to type texts, pick up phone calls and check for new emails? You must coach them to *stop it*! They may think they can handle it all well, but the message they are sending to the person invited into their office is that he/she is not important; in fact, just about *anything* is more important than that individual. If you can't give people your undivided attention, you should negotiate a time to meet when you can.

What if they don't ask; what people just drop in on you? You are not a victim here – you control your time. Let them know you are working on an important deadline, and see if they might reduce their message to a bumper sticker that takes 30 seconds or less, send their message via email or come back at an appointed time that works for both of you. Don't just keep working and hope they will get the message! This is simply being rude.

Don't do this to others and don't let others do it to you. You teach people how to treat you through your actions. When someone multi-tasks with you while you are in his/her office or cubicle, politely acknowledge that they must be busy and that you will connect with them again when they are able to focus on the discussion – then walk out.

The truth is that unbecoming phone and email/text behavior is the action of the addicted activity junkie who wants to feel important. We need to teach our teams not to broadcast their addictions and insecurities. There will be time to read texts and emails. Their power to affect change is in the now and in what is happening in this moment; their decision to commit their undivided attention to their most important tasks will reap large rewards for their communication, their relationships, their business and their careers.

4. *Failure to listen and keep an open mind*

Most of us have a running commentary in our minds that describes the world and our place in it, telling us that this view of the world is the "truth." When someone else's version of the "truth" doesn't match ours, we often stop listening, close our body language and start preparing our mental rebuttal.

Get desensitized to criticism and welcome opposing points of view. You don't have to agree with or adopt these viewpoints, but you do have to understand them if you are to learn and take advantage of others' experience. All of us are smarter than one of us. Learn to adopt phrases like, "Oh, good, another point of view." Or, "Thank you for having the courage to let me know." Or, "I really appreciate your insight." Note this wisdom from Dale Carnegie:

> **Anyone who takes the time to disagree with you is interested in the same things you are.**

Look for what you have in common. Listen carefully so that you can paraphrase the speaker's view back to that person in your *own* words and to *their* satisfaction. This doesn't mean that you agree; it simply means you understand.

Get others to want to have healthy debate with you and to work out conflicts with you in person rather than trashing you in the coffee room with their friends. Simply being open to criticism builds an open, safe environment that allows people to want to talk with you and to be honest, and then you can choose which, if any, opposing views to take to heart.

5. *Failure to employ the "Art of the Question"*

Some of us are so concerned with being right and getting credit for our point of view that we lose sight of the power to help others discover our ideas. As a consultant, I have learned the hard way that you can't *tell* anyone anything; you must help them discover it for themselves. This takes patience, because *telling* is so much faster and easier than employing the art of the question, which is a discovery process that is much more time consuming, but so worthwhile!

The art of the question goes something like the personal coaching outline discussed earlier:

- Know the bumper sticker with which you want to leave them.
- Reverse engineer from there.
- Think through what questions you have to ask to get them to think that bumper sticker in their heads and, even better, say it out loud.

Remember the teacher character from *Peanuts* who taught at the front of the classroom while the students heard only "Wha...wha...wha?" This is how leaders often sound to their teams. People won't really own an idea until they say it aloud. If they arrive at the idea, they will think it's brilliant and will more likely implement it.

Amy was a brilliant, articulate lawyer who found that the partnership/management position she was seeking in the firm was eluding her. She finally asked the partners why, after all her success in the firm, had she not been made the offer of partner. The principals courageously and honestly explained that as partner, Amy would need to manage others effectively and that many had complained of her impatient, condescending and rude style, a situation that would limit her success.

Amy sought my help. Among many of the other tools offered in this chapter, Amy began to employ the art of the question. At one point after practicing this powerful tool, she said, "I have been much better at helping others to arrive at my ideas and I can see that people are responding better to me already. But when do I let them know that the ideas were really *mine*?"

"You don't," I replied. "It doesn't matter."

Leadership mastery is less about being right all the time and more about losing your ego. It's about planting the seeds that help others be right, empowered and accountable. It is worth the time you invest in it to plan your communications so others can discover your view of the world and perhaps even a better one.

Now, remember at the beginning of this section, the person you pictured with whom you have difficult communication? Would you like to be able to disarm them? Try this …

After examining the five biggest obstacles to effective communication in this section, determine those that contribute most to the problem. Then meet with that person and say something like this, "I know our communication isn't very good, and I know that I do a number of things that contribute to the problem. I'm going to work on it (tell them which communication obstacle you plan to work on). Will you meet me half-way and let me know when I fall back to old behaviors?"

Taking the burden of responsibility for poor communication, *even if you don't deserve it*, goes a long way in mending relationships and getting others to want to build a bridge to you.

How to Demonstrate Emotional Intelligence in Five Easy Steps:

Would people rather be understood or agreed with? Numerous studies have shown that people crave the former. Being understood is a deep human need. Many of us don't take the time or don't know how to effectively demonstrate understanding. But I guarantee that throughout your career you have noticed the people who are able to connect with others emotionally – to deeply understand them. You have seen that they consistently communicate more effectively. Their empathy simply gives them the power to get people to open up, share their fears, be genuine and truly listen to them.

Do you know someone who should work on this powerful empathy tool? Often if asked if they'd like to build this skill, such people will say, "You gotta be kidding me. No, I don't want to develop that empathy thing – I just call them like I see them, and I'm not going to mess around trying to do this politically correct stuff." If this sounds like the person you had in mind, you should probably skip to Chapter 8 on Handling Jerks and Conflict. But if you would like to add some empathy tools to your tool-kit, here is a simple, five-step success formula for demonstrating deep understanding through active listening, abridged from Stephen Covey's wonderful *7 Habits of Highly Effective People*:

1. *Ask questions, listen and paraphrase back to them not only*

what they said, but how they feel about it.

Don't say, "I understand." Don't *parrot* their words back to them – which feels like mockery. Demonstrate that you listened and understand it well enough to play it back for them in your own words. Continue to paraphrase until you have been able to say it to their satisfaction. If they hesitate to say that you've got it completely right, repeat until they aren't at all hesitant to say that you've captured it well.

By the way, have you noticed that when people are upset, they continue to tell you about it several different ways, and then drone on, slightly embellishing each version? They are simply trying to get you to understand and they don't believe that you do.

The fastest way to get an upset employee, client, spouse or child to stop telling you their frustrations in a litany of similar statements is to demonstrate that you get it and that you know how they feel – but you must be able to state it to their satisfaction. This takes deep listening skills.

Many leaders are reluctant to take this step because they feel that agreement is implied. It is not. In fact, powerful paraphrase is one of the easiest and most powerful tools available to any leader, parent or spouse. Try it out at home and see the remarkably positive reactions you will receive! They frequently won't recognize what you're doing exactly, but they will know that they like it. Just remember, no judgment, sarcasm or advice – just practice playing back what *they* say and feel.

2. *Watch for the downfall of autobiographical listening!*

We need to eliminate phrases like, "I know just how you feel." (The receiver of that statement is almost always thinking, "No, you don't!") And we must avoid saying, "When it happened to me, it was so much worse!"

These statements make it all about us, and when people are upset they want it to be about *them*. We shouldn't do this with our kids either – you know, the "Back when I was a kid, I had to walk 10 miles to school in the snow, uphill, blah, blah, blah." They stop listening immediately. (You shut off when your parents did it to you, right?)

3. *Don't offer advice until they ask.*

People will not listen to your advice until you have demonstrated deep understanding of what they believe is their highly unique situation. When you launch into advice before truly understanding their uniqueness, they find it insulting and simply tune you out. You will know when you have paraphrased effectively, because they will actually ask you what you think they should do.

If they don't ask, that's okay too. Once you have summarized their problem and feelings to their satisfaction, and they *don't* ask for your advice, simply ask them the most empowering question in the world: "So, what are you going to do?" This question shows that you trust in their ability to solve their own problem and that you don't feel you have to rescue them. The question works great with family, too.

4. *Watch your tone and body language.*

A famous UCLA university study was able to quantify the impact of any given speaker's content, tone and body language on what was actually heard, finding only 7% attributable to content, 38% to tone and a whopping 55% attributable to body language. Yet when we practice difficult communications in the mirror, what do we practice most? Content. How do you practice tone and body language? The answer is that you don't. You can't practice tone and body language, you must actually *feel* the emotions you are trying to convey, or tone and body language will betray your true feelings every time. For example...

If you are *angry*, people will know it. You can count on whatever you do out of uncontrolled anger to serve your needs poorly. So what can you do if you are angry? The truth is that most of our personal and professional anger issues don't involve life or death situations. Buy yourself some time to calm down and plan your approach.

Say to the listener without a hint of anger or sarcasm, "This is important. I'll have to think about that. Can I get back to you in an hour... tomorrow... next week?" Buy whatever time you can. In the interim, walk around the block or go to the gym. Write down every rotten thing you'd like to say to this person about this situation. Do *not* send it – *ever!* Just spilling it from your mind to the page or computer is not only cathartic and mind clearing, but it also helps you gain perspective so you can see through to a more sane and logical approach.

If you are *scared*, your tone and body language will betray you every time. Want a real-life example of how fear can stop you in your tracks and how you can learn to overcome it? Here is one of my most embarrassing stories...

Years ago, as the newly named young president of a company that was hemorrhaging money and the only female executive of the parent company's senior team, I was justifiably asked to present to the Board my plan for turning the company around.

As I stood in the hall outside the carved mahogany doors of the conference room waiting to be summoned to make my presentation, I knew I had the *content* of my message down cold. I knew exactly what was necessary to turn the company to profitability quickly. However, I was pretty intimidated by the setting as well as the celebrity of the successful executive team, and my knees were literally knocking.

I knew I had to get my tone and body language under control, but just couldn't seem to muster the confidence to *feel* it. Finally, the doors creaked open and someone inside said, "You may enter, Ms. Merrill," after which I am mortified to say... wait for it... I fainted! Mind you, when you faint, you don't gently slump to the floor like you see in the movies. Quite the contrary. You hit like a board whatever is in your way on the way down. Long story short, I suffered a mild concussion and clearly failed in my attempt to instill confidence in the board regarding their new president. I was quick to let them know that I hadn't been feeling well, but there is no escaping the inevitable.

Sure enough, a month later, I was standing outside those darn mahogany doors again, waiting to be summoned for my presentation.

Here is the tool I used to manage my fear:

Visualize success and practice your self-talk. Think of your "golden moment." All of us have had them. Think of a time when everything you said turned to gold. You got the reaction you were looking for. Everything you had to say resonated with your audience. Your desired result was achieved.

Have that moment in your tool kit and pull it out when you need it. Re-live that moment and pretend that the audience you are afraid of is actually that golden audience. Use the confidence you feel to present clearly and succinctly. It worked for me. The senior team was impressed, appreciative, and rarely questioned my plans going forward.

Watch for another body-language error: If you have *no respect* for the person you are talking to don't kid yourself. The person knows it. Remember the faces of those people with whom you have difficult communication? I'm guessing that when you try to talk to them, there is a running stream of commentary in your head about what jerks they are. That jerk "feeling" will come through in your tone and body language.

Find something to admire about them. And don't tell me that they don't have any redeeming qualities. Everyone has his/her own "highest and best" attributes worthy of admiration. Find them. Write them down to remind yourself if you have to. Have the discipline to think about those admirable qualities when you talk with each difficult person. Your demeanor will change appreciably, and tough communications will go better.

We can't wait for people to change to fit our style. We can only change ourselves. Anyone who has been married has figured this one out. Our frame of mind and what we are actually feeling make all the difference in tone and body language.

Manage the powerful components of communication tone and body language, and your message will come across as you intend, each and every time.

5. *Mirror their tone and body language.*

People feel safer when speaking with someone they perceive to be like themselves and they will open up when they feel that bond of similarity. The fastest way to demonstrate that similarity is literally to mirror their tone, stance, body language and level of intensity.

If they are sitting forward with their hands folded, do the same. If they are leaning back casually with arms relaxed, do the same. If they are speaking softly, do the same. If they are speaking enthusiastically with animation, do the same.

You get the idea. When your communication, no matter how perfect the content, is out of sync with the listener's tone and body language signals, they feel uncomfortable and they want to escape. Make it easy for them to feel comfortable with you and to trust you. Mirroring effectively takes just a little conscious practice. Try it out at home!

The world's business environment has evolved over the years such that leaders with demonstrated Emotional Intelligence or EQ frequently succeed over those with high IQ and proven experience but a weaker "bedside manner." Add this important skill to your team's tool kit, and they will spend less time swimming upstream and more time building the strong relationships required of a successful career.

As you have seen demonstrated in this chapter, powerful communication skills cover many facets. You are probably performing most of them well already. However, if you feel that you are weaker in any one of these areas (and we all usually have at least one), it will take just a little focus and attention on your part to turn it to a strength.

Summary and Action Steps:

1. Choose just one of the sections in this chapter that you believe most important to taking your communication skills up a notch, such as managing your manager, ensuring that you are actually heard, ensuring healthy debate or avoiding communication obstacles.
2. Highlight that section and practice the steps for correcting that one issue.
3. Practice at home and with friends (if applicable) but definitely at work until you have turned it into communication strength.
4. Tell people the skill you are working to improve and ask them for honest feedback on how you are doing. You'll be surprised at how quickly people

will react to your communications in an even more positive way.

5. Coach your team on how these communication tools can work for them.

Communication – the Bumper Sticker from George Bernard Shaw: "The single biggest problem in communication is the illusion that it has taken place."

8

Secret 7 – Handling Jerks and Conflict

The Conflict Management Guidebook

I used to believe that there were truly nasty, unlikable people in the world. However, after providing in-depth consulting to thousands of people who have bared their souls to me, I learned I was wrong. In my entire consulting career, I have yet to work with a single individual that I didn't like or care about personally. Learning that most people are likeable and trying to do the right thing is one of the most valuable learning experiences I have had as a consultant, and for that I am most grateful.

However, I am frequently hired to do something about the "jerks" in a client's office. For many kinds of coaching sessions, but especially when I know that I've been called in to help a client handle a difficult employee, I use a preliminary 360 evaluation, as mentioned throughout this book. It is an effective tool to help me prepare a perceived jerk to listen to truth as his or her team sees it, perceptions which in effect become that person's reality.

360 evaluations and feedback usually surface recurring themes for these problem employees that sound something like this: *abusive, arrogant, obnoxious, condescending, rude, self-serving, mean and abrasive.* These evaluations are usually conducted prior to my meeting the participant in person. However, I can predict with almost absolute certainty that the "jerks" being described by their associates and co-workers are the most insecure people in the workplace, in the most pain and the most confused about how to change their lot in life. Usually I find that

these very jerks are terrific people and easy to work with because they truly want to understand why their lives aren't turning out as they had hoped.

You will learn much more in this chapter about the potential for a well-conducted 360 to impact behavioral change in a positive way. This chapter will also outline specifically what you can do about the difficult people in *your* work environment as well as what to do about people who are truly toxic. But first, we need to discuss the underlying motivations that drive us *all*.

There are only two real motivators: Love and Fear

From love comes energy, enthusiasm, optimism, creativity, joy, peace, wisdom and compassion. From fear comes worry, anger, jealousy, doubt, greed and insecurity. When you see these negative traits in people, you can safely bet that they are coming from a place of fear. In fact, the people displaying them are actually broadcasting their insecurity.

No one wants to be truly bad or intends evil. Even when they do things perceived by others as evil, they feel justified because of their own perceptions of past wrongs and hurts. Note this from Dale Carnegie's iconic *How to Win Friends and Influence People:*

> **The fact is that all people you meet have a high regard for themselves and are fine and unselfish in their own estimation.**

When you realize that another person's "mistreatment" of you has nothing to do with you and has everything to do with that individual's own pain and frustration, it is much easier not to take the negative actions personally and to offer constructive, compassionate support for the person.

That's actually the point of this chapter – how to get at the "fine and unselfish" person that these people believe they are and want to be, to help them see the disconnect in how they are perceived by those around them and to want to *do* something about that disconnect.

Making a "jerk" see that he is acting like a jerk can be difficult, especially when he continually acts like one toward *you*. When you are being attacked, undermined, manipulated or harassed at work, it is difficult to take the higher road to look for the "fine and unselfish." Remember the section on mirroring in the last chapter? People have a tendency to mirror another person's attitude. When a jerk comes from a place of anger or fear and covers it with aggressiveness or bravado, people dealing with him or her have a tendency to react in kind. Real power comes from rising above that natural instinct and to instead address the pain. Before we review how to do this though, you must first be aware of the "toxic victim."

Toxic Victims – Danger, Danger, Will Robinson!

There will always be people in this world who are simply toxic. For whatever reason, they just are. You can't get through to them, you can't help them, and they will actively work to hurt you or suck you dry emotionally. These are the "victims of life." I don't mean people to whom bad things have happened. Rather I mean those for whom life in total is just one long, horrible ordeal that has been inflicted upon them, in return for which they must seek endless revenge or reassurance. They feel no ownership of their lives, their choices or their outcomes, and they must blame others. Anyone will do. Blaming others for their horrible lot in life is easier than taking ownership of how their lives have actually turned out.

I made a choice long ago not to have toxic victims as clients. As a coach, you can't help them, since they don't want or believe they *need* help. After all, it's not *they* who are the problem; it's everyone else, right? They deflect all needed corrective actions and remedies to someone else... someone you are not coaching... a losing battle.

But some of us aren't that lucky. The "toxic victims" can be our managers, our coworkers, our parents, our spouses, our family members – someone we can't easily carve out of our lives. What are the options?

Unfortunately, there are only three options – well, actually, two and a half.

> ## You can take them, you can leave them or you can change them.

But didn't I just say you *can't* change them? Thus the "half" part of two and a half:

Option 1: Take them. This is a decision to neutralize... to tolerate the victim in your life but not to let him or her hurt you. You see them for exactly who they are, with all their dramas, complaints, neediness and rudeness. Here's the secret. You become a translator in your head. You translate their comments not as personal attacks but rather as depressing reminders of the sad mess they will continue to make of the rest of their lives.

You don't need to defend or react to their bad behavior. Just feel sorry for them. It is difficult for a victim to hurt or abuse you while you are feeling sympathetic. But if you take this approach, be careful not to get caught up in their dramas. Don't engage in their stories and try to "fix them," only to feel depressed and inadequate when you can't. Do everything you can to minimize contact, and when the inevitable contact occurs, let their spew of pain wash *over* you rather than *through* you.

Become skilled at saying things like, "Oh, that must be difficult." OR "How awful for you." OR "I'm sorry to hear that." OR, better yet, "I hate to cut this important conversation short, but I'm running late for my next appointment!"

Option 2: Leave them. This is the best way to deal with toxic victims. Cut these people out of your life. If it is a friend, neighbor, a peer or someone with whom you can legitimately part ways, do it! You know you've been with someone toxic when after contact you consistently feel depleted, exhausted, insecure and spent. It is not only okay to walk away it is the healthy thing to do.

Some of us have to make this choice even with family members when "taking them" becomes so toxic that it interferes with our productive lives. Just stop seeing them. Stop making time for them in your life. Most of the time, they won't even ask why. You will not be the first person in their lives to have taken this action, and at some level they know why you are avoiding them. They won't want their suspicions confirmed. If they do ask why, tell them the truth. Say, "I found that after spending time with you I would feel sad and pessimistic about life. That's just not who I choose to be."

Option 2.5: Change them. This is a tough one and only works if you get them to want to change. Thus, it only gets a half point because few toxic victims *want* to look inward. Note another gem from Dale Carnegie:

> **There is only one way to get people to do anything;**
> **they have to *want* to do it. Remember, there is no other way.**

I am not a psychologist nor am I a therapist. I have no qualifications here whatsoever. But I have had limited success with two lay approaches to getting a toxic victim to change:

1) Arrange a group intervention. Get the people who care about the toxic victim to agree to a surprise meeting with him or her in person and to write prior to that session a heartfelt letter to the "victim" outlining the negative impact he or she is having on their own lives and the lives of their loved ones. During the group meeting, each participant reads his/her letter aloud to the victim. Much like the 360 process, this can work to get the person out of denial. The goal is to have the victim understand that he or she must seek professional support in order to move forward with any kind of happy and productive life.

It is highly suggested that you involve a counselor who can advise you on the preparation for and facilitation of such an emotionally charged session. This work takes great courage on the part of the participants, but the ones who decide to do it usually feel they won't be able to preserve the relationship with the victim any other way, so there is really not much to lose. Plus, it might just help.

Note: Do not try this in the workplace! This is for family and friends only.

2) Confront the victim about his or her beliefs that are driving the toxic behavior. Your thoughts and beliefs drive your actions and results, so you can help the victim take a good, hard look at those beliefs. I offer you here a real-life example.

For nine years, I have mentored a wonderful young woman from the foster care system. We'll call her Cheryl. She was 13 when we first met. Sullen, insecure and harboring rage at her treatment in childhood, Cheryl presented as a dark, gothic, tattooed, pierced girl while at the same time demonstrating a soft, sweet, caring person inside who worried openly if anyone would ever truly love her.

She was also highly manipulative. She used. She lied. She frequently threatened suicide. I got caught up in her pain and enabled her not only with money and "things," but also with instant attention from me whenever she needed it. My behavior only made hers worse. My first three years with her were all about drama. I got a call almost daily with yet another tearful story about how her life "sucked" and how everyone was against her.

Cheryl refused to take responsibility for her life and blamed everyone and anyone handy, including me, for her pain. I hated to write her off as a toxic victim, so three years into the relationship I tried this belief-confrontation approach as a last resort.

Over coffee at a local Starbucks, I asked Cheryl to write down her beliefs about life, God, family, happiness, relationships, etc., and was surprised to find that she wrote tearfully but energetically for about 20 minutes. She filled pages of heartfelt, heart-breaking truths for her. They started something like this:

"God hates me. He is the bully in the playground with the magnifying glass and I am the bug. My life sucks and someone owes me for that."

I read each statement carefully and finally took a deep breath. I said, "I had no idea it was this bad. But, you know, these beliefs are driving your actions, and therefore your outcomes. Is there any chance these beliefs might be wrong?"

"What do you mean?" she snapped. "Like which ones?"

"Well, let's just take the first few. What if God wants what's best for you – wants you to heal, have joy and thrive? What if your life is 100% a result of the choices you've made in it?"

She looked at me with incredulous eyes and said, "Are you saying that my S@#! life is *my* fault?"

"Oh, I don't think it has anything to do with fault," I replied. "I just believe it's all about choices. So let's look at a few of the S@#! things that have happened to you in the last few years."

I asked her to list some of her low points, upon which she wrote, "failing and/ or dropping classes, fights with roommates, unhealthy relationships with boys, gaining weight…"

I then asked, "Was it you or your abuser who made the choices that caused these things to happen?"

With that, she started to sob. When the crying subsided, she started listing other things for which she had always blamed others. After each she asked, "So this is my fault? That is my fault?"

Encouraging her to get away from the "fault" word, I said, "What was the choice that caused it to happen and who made that choice?"

As she went through every scenario, she quickly came to the conclusion that her abuser had stopped making decisions about her life years ago. She now owned her choices along with the power to make different ones.

Oh, how painful at the age of 16 to accept full responsibility for one's life! Cheryl showed amazing courage and was remarkably able within minutes to look at her life without excuses and to choose a different path forward. How many 50-year-olds are unable to display that kind of courage?

That's why this approach represents only half an option in "taking, leaving or changing" a toxic victim. Confronted with this kind of responsibility, a toxic victim will most often shift blame and fail to claim ownership or responsibility for their lives. Not Cheryl.

I continue to get frequent calls from her, but none complaining about how life is conspiring against her. Cheryl now focuses on analyzing her options at every crossroads and deciding which choice she will make. She doesn't always make healthy choices, but they are now conscious choices. I love Cheryl, and am delighted that I continue to receive these calls from such a responsible young adult. I will be her mentor for as long as she needs me to be one. We all need mentors!

I went to some length to explain toxic victims here so we could examine the limited possibilities for dealing with them. But please don't make the mistake of putting all the "difficult" people in your life in this toxic victim category. That would be too easy. As I said at the beginning, most people – even when troubled and acting from fear – are likeable and able to heal. Most people aren't pathologically toxic. However, their bad behaviors can still disrupt and cause mayhem in your life. How do you deal with *those* types of people?

10 Secrets to Handling Difficult People:

1. *Change YOUR thoughts and beliefs.* The difficult person at work or at home is usually not your competitor or enemy but rather your partner or family member. Let go of whatever has bugged you about this person in the past. If it's a coworker, the organization has kept this person on for a reason. Look for the positive reasons. The family member has something to offer. Look for it. What could you and this person do to make life better for both of you? Find it! Pay attention to the best in this person and stop trashing him or her in your head.

2. *Prepare yourself before meeting with the "difficult."* Outline the vital points you need from this relationship. Which boundaries or changed behaviors are required for the two of you to work or be together? Know the bumper sticker that you would like the person to be able to say if the conversation goes well. Be ready to reverse engineer. And be prepared with what you "think" *their* bumper sticker for you might be, but lose your attachment to your preconceptions.

   When you think about this difficult person, you need to feel calm or your tone and body language will betray you, as we discussed in the last chapter. By clearly understanding your position and attempting to truly understand the other person's, you can begin to think of ways to build bridges rather than continuing the war.

3. *Be the bigger person.* Swallow your pride, take full responsibility for the status of the relationship and apologize, even if you don't believe the problems are your fault. Being the "bigger person" is about being able to take full blame, even when it truly wasn't your fault.

   Need an example? Think of someone you work with right now with whom you may not have an ideal relationship. Let's start there. You might say, "I know we got off to a bad start and that our relationship isn't as effective as it should be. We are operating as competitors in silos rather than partners with a mutual goal to grow the business, and I take full responsibility for where we are right now. I apologize and want to work with you to create a dynamic environment between our teams that achieves great results. Would you be willing to help me with that?" If you try this approach, how do you think he or she might react?

4. ***Get them saying yes.*** The next step is to explain your position. While doing so, talk to the highest and best part of that person... not the part that makes you angry. Identify gaps, but look for where you are in agreement first. Get both of you saying yes. Then tackle the more difficult issues. Here is an example:

"Matt, would you agree that your team is working hard to increase sales? That your team can have only limited success without the enthusiastic support of my team? That working against each other is hurting us both? That we can get more done working together than when fighting for credit?"

5. ***Use "Aikido."*** I know. It might sound like a small dog breed, but Aikido is a martial art designed to use your opponent's strength against him. You are taught in this discipline to push when your opponent pulls and to pull when your opponent pushes. Doing the physically unexpected throws him or her off balance. The same is true emotionally. Do the emotionally unexpected! Do more than agree with your difficult person. As you prepared in Step 2, *initiate* the other person's point of view before he or she brings it up and then take it a step further. Try to state your opponent's position to his or her satisfaction as if you were trying to talk yourself out of your position. Ask if you have it right and lose the sarcasm!! Get that position to a bumper sticker that your opponent can enthusiastically endorse. Remember that you don't have to agree with this statement; you simply must *understand* it!

6. ***Don't get down in the dirt.*** Stay focused on mutual goals – see if you can agree on the problem or goal. It is so much easier to agree on positive next steps if you agree on what you are trying to accomplish together. Look for the noble goal that would allow you both to win and which would be so exciting that you could ignore petty differences if you were able to accomplish it. Try something like, "What if we could increase sales by 20% if we worked together?"

7. ***Brainstorm solutions together.*** Now that you agree on the goal, ask what we haven't tried that would make this goal possible? No idea is lame. You could say something like, "Let's just throw out as many as we can think of." Offer suggestions and listen to the other person's.

Here is an example: "What if we share credit, align incentives, establish audacious goals for both our teams to increase sales by 20% by end of this fiscal year? What if we create a high-level, dedicated team to work with your team to take innovative actions for penetrating key accounts? Could we offer a special joint celebration if this goal is achieved?"

8. *Paraphrase frequently.* Whether this difficult person is a boss, peer, subordinate or family member, you have the power to listen and to get to the heart of what is bothering him or her. Paraphrase until you have that person's bumper sticker down to the individual's satisfaction. Give the person a chance to have some space with you not to defend or explain, but simply to vent and get it off his or her chest.

9. *Don't be intimidated.* For those who use intimidation, remember that they are operating from a place of fear. They have learned that making others fearful takes the pressure off their own insecurity. Intimidation is a habit that works, so they expect people to cower and are actually scornful of them when they do. Again, act in unexpected ways. Just like the bully on the playground, intimidators go after the easy target. Don't be one. Be calm, relaxed, bored and/or amused. If you actually want to try to change them, be aggressive. Bullies back down when confronted.

10. *Use 360s.* If you have the power to do so, arrange for them, or even better both of you, to participate in an objective and anonymous 360 evaluation. As explained throughout this book, this is an excellent tool to help people see themselves objectively without excuses. Remember those nasty recurring themes I told you about at the beginning of the chapter… "abusive, arrogant, obnoxious, condescending, rude, self-serving, mean, abrasive?" When delivering 360 results to participants with this kind of feedback, I always use the "Seven-Step Formula for Coaching" as outlined in Chapter 5:

> *Step 1: Preparing yourself.* After reading all the anonymous comments, I look for the recurring themes both in strengths and weaknesses, and put into two or three bumper stickers the areas they most need to work on to become even more effective or prevent career derailment, so I can reverse engineer my line of questions. Why only the recurring themes? Because isolated comments are often damaging and inflammatory. It is where multiple people say the same thing that the

truth lies. Also, when multiple people say the same thing, it is easy to maintain anonymity.

Step 2: Preparing the person being coached. I read to the participant slowly and with sincerity the amazing list of genuine strengths offered about them by the respondents. This list always outweighs the weaknesses, and they are usually detailed and heartfelt. This step relaxes the person and lets them know that the 360 process is not about attack.

Step 3: Delivering the message. With no sugarcoating, I read the list of comments that support the recurring theme weaknesses I identified in preparation, without including anything that would identify a specific respondent. That reading might go something like, "He is rude, he doesn't listen, he always sees his own priorities as more important than anyone else's, self-serving, doesn't listen, has to have his own way, never listens, takes over every conversation, bullies people, never hears your message, doesn't try to understand, thinks he knows it all, condescending, doesn't listen, starts every conversation with 'I've done this before and know what I'm doing.'"

Remember to be supportive. While delivering this "reading," I am careful to have a gentle tone and to do nothing with body language that implies anything but genuine support for the participant – absolutely no judgment or anger. Remember, these people are coming from fear.

Step 4: Asking for replay. I then ask, "What did you hear?" I don't try to summarize for them, put words in their mouths or tell them what they should do to improve. At this point, I simply want the participant to say the bumper sticker for him or herself. Maybe it will be something like, "I guess I need to listen better." It is difficult for the participant to deny the problem when he or she hears it from 14 different people in slightly different ways. Rarely after such a reading do the participants replay something disconnected from the reading such as, "I guess I need to manage my *time* better." But if they do, I simply repeat the reading and ask again for the replay.

Step 5: Agreeing on a clear goal. At this point, I ask the participant to write a clear, succinct and noble goal that would address the bumper sticker that he or she stated above, starting with, "I will..." For example, "I will be an excellent listener." OR "I will welcome and value others' ideas and suggestions."

Step 6: *Creating a contract.* Now we brainstorm together. What might the participant do specifically to achieve this goal? We both offer ideas, and none of them can be considered lame. Then the participant writes down the action steps he or she is willing to implement with due dates for when they will be achieved. I offer tools, options and suggestions, but the participant must own these written steps if they are to be taken seriously. We talk about what will happen if he or she follows through. We also talk about what the future will be like if the person doesn't.

Step 7: *Establishing follow through.* I ask the participants to summarize what they have learned and what they plan to do next. This is where we can catch any blame-shifting or lack of sincerity about what needs to be done, which rarely happens.

I then give the following instructions on how to treat the respondents who completed their 360 assessments when they return to the office:

Thank the people who gave you input. You don't know who completed the assessments and who didn't. Thank all those on your distribution list anyway. It took courage to complete those forms – they didn't know for sure how confidential the material would be kept. If you found the feedback helpful, at least let your colleagues know that you appreciated the time they invested to give it to you honestly. (And those who didn't complete the feedback will feel guilty!)

I know you wouldn't do this, but please don't spend a second trying to determine who said what or, even worse, chastise anyone for what was said. This not only undermines the process but it makes you look insecure.

If you have courage, share with those on your distribution list that as a result of their input you established two important leadership growth goals. If you have real courage, tell them what the goals are!

If you have off-the-charts courage, ask them to call you on it real-time when you fall back to old behaviors and fail to follow through with your commitments for growth (it happens to all of us).

The above steps create an accountability system. If you are serious about these goals, the more people you tell about your intent to follow through on them, the more accountable you will be. Be like a smoker who is willing to tell her friends that she is quitting so she knows they will hold her accountable if she lights up. Be unlike the one who doesn't want to tell anyone, because she wants the flexibility to be able to light up again without judgment or criticism. Which of the two is more likely to quit? Enlist your accountability partners.

But at minimum, thank the respondents on your distribution list.

Literally hundreds of my clients have taken these courageous steps toward frank vulnerability and openness to change. Many are fearful that in being this transparent, they will appear weak. On the contrary! The amazing people who have taken these steps have found that even lifelong enemies soften, rally round them and work to support them simply because they have had the courage to apologize and commit to change. Some "opponents" even become friends.

I have seen hundreds of executives get positive, often life-changing results with this process. You should also know that although I have liked and personally cared about them all, I have yet to find a perfect person. We *all* have things to work on. The 360 evaluation can help anyone look honestly and objectively at what those lesser strengths are so they can decide if they want to do something about them. Knowledge is power and once you know better, you can do better.

The 360 process is one of the most powerful tools in my consulting tool belt and I have gone to some length here to show you how the process can work to help difficult people own the disconnect between who they perceive themselves to be and how others perceive them.

However, I highly recommend that you don't try the 360 process on your own. Effective 360s require extensive training and when done badly, even with the right intentions, they can cause even more emotional damage to the participant, while fracturing relationships and splitting teams. If you choose this approach, secure a qualified facilitator who can demonstrate a safe, nurturing process and offer testimonials indicating consistently positive outcomes. You may have such a person in your own company.

You'll find difficult people in every facet of life. It's often frustrating to learn that they don't believe *themselves* to be difficult. But it is comforting to know that their negative behavior comes from fear, and to the extent you can be the bigger person and help to decrease that fear, thus engaging the person they believe themselves to be, you can usually build stronger, more productive relationships with almost anyone.

Summary and Action Steps:

1. Understand that negative, pain-inflicting behavior always comes from a place of fear.
2. Identify toxic victims and eliminate them from your life if you can.
3. Don't take the easy way out and categorize all difficult people as toxic victims. They usually aren't.
4. Choose a difficult person in your life with whom you would like to have a better relationship. Review the 10 Steps above for handling difficult people. Which steps would work to take your relationship with this person to a healthier level?
5. Don't wait for difficult people to change. Be the bigger person, listen deeply, initiate healthy actions that allow you to help such people push past their fears and build mutually beneficial goals.

Handling Difficult People – the Bumper Sticker: Leadership is about unlocking the potential of the fine and unselfish person everyone believes themselves to be.

9

Secret 8 - Time is Everything!

How to make time because you won't find it

Poor time management costs most leaders an average of two hours per day, which equates to 20 working days or one month a year. Could you use an extra month?

I have been hired by CEOs on many occasions just to help them find more time. The sad truth is that you have 100% of all the time there is. I cannot magically create more time for you. Even if I were to have those powers, I'm betting you would still need more.

You have the same amount of time as do kings, presidents, popes and celebrities. There are 24 hours in a day and seven days in a week. You won't *find* time. You have to make it. But how do you *make* time?

In this chapter, you will learn specific tools for becoming a master at prioritization and to manage the time you have!

Do You Manage Time or Does Time Manage You?

Give yourself the following yes-or-no time-management quiz and see how far down the list you can continue to say *yes*:

- Do you have a to-do list that includes all of your commitments?
- Are they all on one list rather than on numerous PostIt™ notes stuck on refrigerators, bookshelves, phones, laptop etc.?

- Does the list include both business and personal commitments?
- Do you have an updated calendar of all meetings and appointments?
- Do you update both the list and the calendar at the end of the day *before* leaving the office?
- Are all items on your to-do list in priority order?
- Do you know clearly the top three most important things you will need to do tomorrow *before* you leave the office today?

If you said yes all the way down the list, congratulations! You are managing your time pretty well and you are in the top 5% of all executives in the country as it relates to time management!

If you said *no* to some or many of the questions above, you are not alone. Let me predict a typical day in your life…

You walk into your office in the morning with your cup of coffee, finding stacks of papers, projects, folders, notes and emails on your desk, in the computer, on the credenza and sometimes on the floor and chairs around your desk. These are the same projects, papers, notes, etc., that were there the night before, plus a few nasty new additions to the stacks. You sift through the documents as you look for the biggest grenades, eager to embark on that which is most urgent, reminding yourself in the process of those items you should have completed a week ago.

With a sense of angst and a lot of hope you begin to tackle those about which you feel most guilty. Someone pops into your office to discuss a new problem, your manager offers you a new deadline, you react to a pending crisis… and all of a sudden it's 5 o'clock in the afternoon, your coffee is cold and you haven't made any progress on the guilt project that you started this morning. Now it's time for the big decision: do you stay late and finally get something done, incurring the wrath of your family, or do you go home and try to make more progress tomorrow?

The time-management truth is the same for everyone. We all need to manage our time or face working late hours to catch up on things we should have been able to accomplish during business hours. If you face the choice of working late or into the wee hours of the morning more often than you would like, you need to manage your time. If you want to learn how to be a true time wrangler, keep reading. You must become a prioritization-pro, and warning… you might have to eat a frog.

Mastering Prioritization

Let's go back to the time-management quiz. That is the formula for success. Use the bullet items to guide you. When you can answer *yes* to all questions in that quiz, you will be managing your time effectively. Here is how to get to 100% yes…

Have two documents with you at all times: An updated *calendar* and an updated *to-do* list.

The updated calendar should include *all* meetings and appointments. As for the to-do list, gather everything from your desk and any other surface in your office that represents work yet to be done. Then transfer all this information to a to-do list that includes *all* of your commitments (throwing out the ancient ones that linger there). If you haven't been diligent about this in the past, it may take several hours to get this single list together. But once it's done you can let your to-do list manage your time rather than the stacks in your office!

Get everything on *one* list. Microsoft Office has a great task manager, and you can upload it to your computer, your iPad and your phone. You can even use the "hardcopy-saurus" version – if that works better for you. Either way, have a version that is available to you all day every day.

For both calendar and to-do list, be sure to include both business and personal commitments. There is only one of you – don't try to double book yourself. Spend 10 minutes updating both documents at the end of each day before leaving your office.

Get your to-do list in priority order! At minimum, know the top ten items that must get done. As outlined by Stephen Covey's *7 Habits of Highly Effective People*, here's how to do that with skill:

- Label all urgent-crises-deadline-fire-drill-focused items on your to-do list as MED (medium priority). These are the items that demand your greatest attention and which keep you in reactive mode. Most executives spend the majority of their time here. Spending most of your time here dooms you to continue to spend most of your time here, because you aren't doing anything to prevent these fire drills. Using Pareto's 80/20 rule, you should spend only 20% of your time here, because this work yields inconsequential results over the long term.

- Label all strategic-coaching-planning-training-procedural-focused items on your to-do list as HI (high priority). Few executives spend enough time here. This is the proactive mode where you will find your highest and best use and where you should spend 80% of your time. This work will prevent the medium priority crisis items from happening with such frequency and urgency and these HI priority items will yield the 80% result.

- Label everything else LOW (low priority).

Note: Several of my clients actually place their updated to-do list with the HI, MED and LOW priority indications on the door of their office each week, with the following direction to their teams: "If you are coming to talk to me about anything labeled HI priority, you are welcome anytime. If you are coming to talk to me about anything labeled MED priority, come with suggested solutions! If you are coming to talk to be about anything labeled Low priority, go see someone else!"

I often see people walk up to the door, read the list and labels, slump their shoulders and walk away. Isn't that perfect? Tell your people how you want to focus your time and how they should be focusing theirs. Be explicit.

Within this framework of proactive vs. reactive priorities, decide honestly the top 10 on your to-do list. Draw a line under number 10 and see what falls below it. What can be ignored, delegated or delayed? If it can be delegated, put someone's specific name on it and make a plan to hand off responsibility to the appropriate person immediately.

As you do, be sure to give that person both the "what and the why." Tell them what success looks like, why it is important, what will happen if they achieve it and what will happen if they don't. Focus less on *how*!

Know clearly the top three most important things you need to do tomorrow *before* you leave the office today so you will have a solid game plan for tackling your tomorrow. New grenades will inevitably throw you off track, but if you are clear about what three tasks must absolutely be accomplished in a given day, those three priorities will draw you back like a magnet, preventing you from drifting into the next random project that causes you to squander another day.

If you choose your top three well, there will be some tough items on that list – the kind not easily accomplished – and you may be unclear about how to start. You will be tempted to go to the items on your list that are more easily and quickly achieved and those are often more fun. Stay focused on and disciplined about your top three.

And if you work for someone else, when your boss swoops in demanding that you drop everything to handle a new important crisis, say yes immediately and then show her your prioritized to-do list with the top 10 priorities. Ask her to decide where this new assignment falls on the list. Rest assured that most of the items in the top 10 are highly important to your manager, since most of them came from her! Let her negotiate with your list and with herself the importance of the new task relative to the other priorities. This removes much of the stress from your shoulders and allows true alignment with your manager. But it only works if you have done the homework to create a prioritized list in the first place; otherwise, you are asking your manager to do your prioritization work for you, which I warn you can be career-limiting...

For those of you who think your managers are sadistic because of the volume of tasks and projects they continue to throw your way, understand that as soon as the work is assigned and off their list, they have forgotten about it. They certainly don't keep a running tab of all that is accumulating on your list. Your top 10 list is a great reminder for your manager that keeps everything in perspective without drama or emotion.

Sandy, CEO of an interior design company, contacted me a few years ago, explaining that she felt like she was being taken advantage of by her board as well as her team. All crucial issues somehow ended up on her desk, delegated either down or up for resolution. She was working nights and weekends; both her family life and her health were suffering. She struggled with guilt when she was home because of all that was left unresolved at work. She struggled with guilt at work because of the family events and memories she felt she was missing. She no longer had time for fitness and she was gaining weight. She was miserable and asked me to help her stop the abuse and "fix the people on her team."

We started by implementing the daily discipline of identifying three vital work and three critical home issues that would win her time. Once identified, ignoring these issues was non-negotiable. Anything else could be ignored, delayed or delegated. There is a huge relief in just making this single decision daily! Sandy also used several of the following tools in this chapter, but the end result of choosing well her top three priorities for the day paid off for her big time. She worked fewer hours, got more meaningful work accomplished, and spent quality time with her family. It wasn't her team or her Board causing her to lose out on her life; it was her lack of focus... the choices she made. In a nutshell, the problem was Sandy.

If you feel like Sandy, rest assured that you have the power to change things. Be diligent about prioritizing both your personal and business life – every day. When you agonize about long lists of things, believing that *all* of them must be done, have the discipline to condense, to simplify and *focus*.

Don't try to shoehorn every activity that comes your way into your day. Keep it simple. Choosing not to deal with some of the incoming isn't failure. You are barraged with *incoming* all day long. Determine quickly if what comes in actually fits into the vital or trivial bucket and prioritize the most vital. If it helps, visualize two buckets. One has *Vital* scrolled across its side; the other displays *Trivia*. The *Vital* bucket can only hold three items. Have no more than three important issues a day on which you *will* make progress. You will be happier, healthier, calmer, more productive and more successful. Not bad for simply focusing on what Pareto learned 150 years ago.

We spent a lot of time on prioritization here. That is because it is the single most essential tool for managing your time. If you use the prioritization tools outlined here to consistently prioritize your "incoming," you will be more purposeful and will consistently achieve the 20% that yields the 80% result! And now for that frog...

Why You Should Eat a Frog

Imagine that two young boys, hoping to be accepted into a prestigious social club, are challenged with a difficult task during an initiation ceremony. They are both told that they must eat a grilled frog as the final rite of passage into the club. One boy, feeling the task is disgusting but knowing that a cooked frog won't hurt him, dives at his frog, tearing off pieces and stuffing them into his mouth. His frog is gone within seconds.

The other boy stares at the ugly critter for hours, procrastinating the inevitable and wishing for another way out. He makes himself nauseous over the offensive creature. However, highly motivated to join his friends in the club, he begins to eat it slowly in tiny, agonizing pieces and it takes him all night long.

Which kid suffered more?

When attacking the top three items on your list… eat the frog! Do it quickly – first thing in the morning. Don't procrastinate, lament, worry and delay only to end up having to do the nasty deed anyway. Taking a phrase from Nike™, just do it! That said, you'll have to be mindful of monkeys!

Watching for Monkeys

Perhaps you are familiar with the famous 1999 HBR article "Who's Got the Monkey?" If not, here are the cliff notes:

Some people are skilled at giving their monkeys to someone else for care and feeding. Other people are monkey magnets, reluctant to say no, often accepting other people's responsibilities for the care and feeding of their monkeys. If you could visualize both types of people as they leave the office each day, some are covered head to toe in monkeys, swarming them for food and attention. Others leave the office monkey-free! Which type of worker is most effective?

Actually neither is handling their appropriate responsibilities. The monkey-free folks are over-delegating and not assuming their real responsibilities. Monkey-magnets are people pleasers who have a difficult time saying no, thus jeopardizing their ability to complete their own projects and delaying productivity all around when they are unable to keep up with the workload. We should all own our own projects and tasks and require others to own theirs! And be most careful about your own people tossing you their monkeys. But how can you determine if this is happening?

Spend one day tracking how you spend your time in 15-minute increments. Throughout the day ask yourself, "Would I outsource or hire someone and pay my salary for this work? Is what I am doing right now contributing to my top five success metrics? Is this someone else's monkey?"

By being diligent in deciphering your highest, best and most appropriate use, and focusing your time there, you will create more cushion in your life to achieve that which is most important.

Okay… now that you have a handle on the monkeys in your life, let's take a look at the rest of the herd… 'er, I mean employees and associates.

Herd Ball

Have you ever watched six-year-old children play soccer? If so, you know that the ball seems to be a magnet and the kids act like metal shavings, running in a clump to wherever the ball goes. It's fun to watch when they are six, but you wouldn't want to watch a professional team playing like this. We love to watch the elegant hand-offs of athletes skillfully playing their positions in professional sports. Apply the concept of the professional soccer field to your office.

What kind of company do you figure yours to be? Do people flock to problems, tripping over each other with lots of drama ensuing, while other important matters are neglected? Or are roles, responsibilities and levels of authority clear? Do people know who to go to for what, where to direct incoming calls and when to escalate problems? If not, you and your people could be wasting a great deal of time in redundant effort and sloppy, inefficient workflow.

Publish your organization chart for all "players" to see. Make each person's roles and top responsibilities clear. Consider routing yourself through the office as a new "sold" piece of business might to see where you get held up and where you are efficiently managed. This will help you surface where roles, responsibilities and authority levels are unclear.

This kind of workflow analysis may not have a sense of urgency to it, but it's that high-priority/low-urgency kind of task we talked about earlier that will save you and your team a great deal of unproductive time over the long haul.

Next, take a look at your meetings, emails and phone calls. Do they suck you dry? My clients tell me that they are universal time-robbers. Use the next section to develop your own protocols to arrest them.

Getting Meetings and Emails Under Control

Most of my clients complain about the overwhelming volume of meetings and emails to which they must attend. I have found that often, the largest volume and most onerous of both are generated internally! I advise my clients to take charge of these internal time wasters. Those who are most successful implement some or all of the following *Meeting and Email Rules of Engagement* for their companies, departments or teams (whatever scale they can influence) – and they enforce them.

You can use their experience! Review the following examples and work with your teams to determine which would help you to corral meeting and email monsters – then implement and enforce those, along with any new ones you might devise as a team.

Rules of Engagement for Meetings

- You must have an agenda, delivered at least one day prior to the meeting to include:
  > A meeting leader
  > A one-sentence meeting purpose
  > The location, date, start and stop times
  > Topics to be covered
- You must honor other people's time and show up on time; the meeting will start on time and there will be repercussions for those who are late.
- No electronic devices allowed!
- You will conduct Healthy Debate.
- Meeting Minutes will be kept and distributed, outlining all commitments – who is responsible, what specifically will happen and when.
- You will outline the top five "bumper stickers" that result from the meeting for use in Waterfall Communication to the rest of the staff.

Rules of Engagement for Emails (Examples used to reduce the volume of annoying and unproductive *internal* messaging.)

- All emails must have a subject line clearly identifying the bumper-sticker topic along with an indicator of "Info Only" or "Action Required."
- Never "Reply All" unless your response is necessary for all recipients. (Never reply to multiple people with "Thank you.") Respond only to the original sender.
- If you have constructive criticism to offer someone, you must first talk to that person before emailing him or her or copying others.
- You may not send an email describing a problem to one or many without posing a potential solution and action required.
- Avoid stream of consciousness emails – know your bumper sticker for the message and reverse engineer.
- Let the recipient know your deadline for a response, why you need it and what action you will take if you don't receive their response by that deadline.
- Emails last forever. You don't know how they will be copied, distributed or used. Would you be embarrassed to see your email on the front page of the newspaper or posted in the coffee room? If so, revise or don't send. Your email could end up posted anywhere for all eyes to see. If you are very upset about something, have the cathartic experience of writing it out in email, but by all means, until you can be calm and revise it, do not hit the send button!

As for *external* emails, don't rush to read them each time you hear the incoming beep. Again, you should manage emails; don't let them manage you. Block out two times a day (actually schedule it on your calendar) to read and return essential emails. Using the above protocol, ignore the rest. If you have access to an assistant, teach him or her the criteria for what you consider "essential" emails and offer direction that you receive only those.

You *can* establish policies with your internal team to manage the enormous volume of time-wasting meetings and emails that they generate. You can manage your external volume by identifying and being diligent about what is worthy of your time. Again, this is one of those important and non-urgent, proactive tasks that once accomplished will save you hours each week!

Time-Savers for the Chronically Behind

I've learned many timesaving techniques over the years and will share some of them with you here, but I guarantee that they won't all work for all of you. Choose the ones that *will*:

- Know your top three priorities for the day and eat the frog first!

- Especially for the monkey-magnets, get good at saying no... nicely. The idea is to explain why it is in the delegator's best interest to delegate to someone other than you. For example, you might say, "This project is important. I don't have the time right now to give it the attention it deserves. With all the priorities currently on my plate, it will either be late or done halfway, which neither of us wants. Is there someone else who could give it the time and attention it deserves now?"

- Designate one to two hours each week for private, uninterrupted time for you and your staff – they will love you for it!

- Consult with your team on the biggest time robbers in the office and brainstorm together what you will do together to kill them.

- If phone interruptions are the problem:

  - If not vital, let voicemail answer and return the call when it is convenient for you. Some of us believe that if the phone rings and we are in the office, we have almost a moral obligation to pick up the phone. It isn't true. Unless you are in sales or customer service, most of your incoming calls are not vital. Choose carefully to accept those calls that are more important than the vital, top priority task on which you are working, and decide to return the rest at *your* convenience.

  - Implement voice ID, so you know who is calling.

  - Establish a "quick discussion" expectation up front. You can give the caller a five-minute window, explaining that you are due to leave for a meeting.

- If drop-in visitors are the problem:

  - Make it difficult for them to make eye contact with you (which usually invites interruptions). It's effective for some to have their desk or computer face the wall.

- Remove the extra chairs from your office or cubicle, because they serve to invite visitors. You can't always control your visitor traffic, but you can control your furniture!

- Stand up as uninvited guests enter the room, which sends a signal that your time is short and that you may be on your way to another commitment.

- Work in another office, in the conference room or from home one morning a week. You may be in the office, but they won't be able to find you!

- Don't let social media suck up your day either. Facebook, Twitter, Google +1, YouTube and LinkedIn are valuable but addictive marketing tools. Delegate social media to an assistant or social media professional who can handle the job for the company or prepare yourself for a whole lot of overtime, because social media isn't something you need to be doing unless you are in marketing and sales.

- Are you a pack rat who's built a paper jungle?

  - Only touch paper once. Do it, dump it or delegate it!

  - Imagine opening both email and snail mail over a trash can. Erase or throw away immediately anything you aren't going to do or isn't essential to keep.
    - If you're going to do it, add it to your to-do list with the appropriate priority level.
    - If you're going to dump it eventually why not dump it now?
    - If you're going to delegate a project or task, assign a name to it and delegate it now.

  - Have a great filing system for anything you are going to keep. Focus on having only a few major file categories for both hardcopy and email rather than establishing a new file for every new email or piece of paper. Keeping only a few broad file categories to remember is the only way you will ever find these items again!

- Have only one project on your desk at a time. All that clutter in your peripheral vision only adds to your stress. Organization brings a sense of calm and control.

- Get rid of or archive files and papers that haven't been touched in a year or more, unless you are a financial or legal office (in which case you have to save files for longer periods). If you haven't touched them in that period of time, you likely won't!

- Again, if you are a true pack rat, shredding documents will hurt your soul. So pack up the offending papers in a box and archive them off-site. You'll be getting rid of time-wasting clutter and though you'll probably never again open the box, you'll feel better. Your productivity will likely increase, too.

- Include in your monthly purge your "interesting reading" pile! Be honest. Some of that stuff has been sitting in the same spot for years. Toss anything older than three months in the recycle can and feel good about it.

- The same is true for clothes, by the way. If you haven't worn it in a year, you likely won't. Charities need it. Get rid of the guilt and clutter. Experience the freedom of *less*.

Take a careful inventory of the suggestions in this chapter that will save you time and implement one or two. Using these tools, most of my clients have been able to save at least five hours a week. What would you do with your five hours?

Summary and Action Steps:

1. Have an updated to-do list and calendar with you at all times.
2. Know your priorities and be ruthless in managing where you spend your time.
3. Don't procrastinate. Eat the frog!
4. Be honest. Stop telling yourself that you need to do other people's jobs

for them.

5. Get skilled at saying no nicely. Explain why *no* is in the other person's best interest.
6. Make roles, responsibilities, levels of authority and workflow clear and streamlined.
7. Manage your meetings, emails and workspace – there is real time treasure here.

Time Management – the Bumper Sticker: You have the power to manage time; it doesn't have to manage you!

10

Secret 9 - Delegation Soup... A Recipe for Empowering Others
Quick and easy steps to effective delegation

I have met a lot of crappy delegators. I know one when I see one, because I was one myself! Let's face it. Most of us make it to positions of leadership by being skilled and talented contributors. We excel at what we do, and we figure few in the world can do it as well. It's normal to feel this way, especially when it's your neck on the line, and important projects and reputations are at stake. In such cases, the last thing you want to do is turn over the reins to a direct report who will likely screw it up. At least that is what we tell ourselves.

You know that delegation is important. You control freaks like me are just hoping you can be successful without it. But learning the art of delegation is an absolute necessity for growth, no matter what position you hold. You cannot successfully do all tasks and take on all aspects of all projects all of the time. But how do you artfully delegate?

This chapter will outline nine easy and specific steps to becoming a delegation pro. But first, let's look at your and your team's behavior patterns, for example, what do you do when people bring you their problems to fix?

Do Your People Delegate UP?

Of course they do. Can you think of a manager who puts out fires all day long? I'll bet you can. Let's call her Karen.

Karen's people were hired for their talent, strength, experience and ability to create solutions. So why do they bring their problems to her? She probably says to herself, "Well, it is my job to help them. They need my experience and support. I'm supposed to have the answers, right? They just need my guidance!"

The truth? They bring the problems to Karen because they don't have to think, it's easy, she takes away their accountability when she solves a problem for them (because whether it works or not, they did as she said) *and* she continues to do it!! I don't know why everyone in the company doesn't bring their problems to Karen.

We know why *they* do it; the bigger question is why *Karen* does it. Why does she solve their problems for them? The truth is that the fastest way to get those problems and their owners out of her office is to give them the answers. And if they leave with her answer, could there be a better one? Karen thinks not!

In truth, Karen is doing them and herself a big disservice over the long haul by being the all-knowing problem solver. She is not teaching her people to think. She is not growing her bench strength. She is creating dependent, risk-averse people who know they can lean on her for every major decision. In fact, *she* is the bottleneck that keeps her company and her team from growing and her from achieving work/life balance. Karen needs to note this famous quote and conduct a little self reflection:

> # Please do not feel personally, irrevocably responsible for everything... That's my job.
> # Love, God

Think about it... When Karen is doing everyone else's job for them, when does she have time to do her own? That's what nights and weekends are for, right? And as she works toward burn out during those never-ending nights and weekends, incurring the scorn of her family, she has a tendency to say, "I am sure earning my keep around here. This company is working me to death!" Well who is doing that to her? Hmmm... that would be Karen.

She has reached a crossroads. Someone must tell Karen that her job has changed: "Karen, you are no longer a doer, but a leader of doers. You reached a position of leadership by being a hero. Your new job is to be a *creator* of heroes, and this new job requires a whole different skill set, one that subordinates your ego. You must not only tolerate but encourage others to shine."

Then offer her a way out:

We all know that when people bring us their problems, we're supposed to ask, "So, what do you think you should do?" Most of us don't, though. Why? We'd have to watch them think!! I don't know about you, but I don't have time to watch people think. So here is a solution. Tell your staff and associates that they can come into your office to discuss problems with you anytime, but that they must come with two solutions.

Tell them that they must be prepared with the following:

- The problem summarized in a bumper sticker. Why? Because for them to describe the problem that succinctly, they must truly understand it. Frequently, people actually delegate *up* the diagnosis of the problem as well as the problem itself, offering long and wordy descriptions of all that has gone wrong, without a well-thought through diagnosis of the root cause.

  I must admit, I used to do the same thing in college when I was filling out those blue essay test books. If I knew the answer, I filled out a paragraph or two – just enough to answer the question. If I didn't know the answer, I would regurgitate as much of the textbook as I could remember, hoping something would stick. Your people sometimes do the same thing. Teach them the discipline to arrive at their own diagnoses.

- They should then offer two solutions in bumper sticker formats, along with their recommendation for which solution should be followed and why.

- If they fail to think through their problems and solutions effectively before talking with you and you find yourself watching people think, ask them to commit the above to writing to one short page before coming in to see you again on an issue.

What would happen if Karen reinforced this process religiously? I'll tell you what happened to Frank, a CEO who felt he could spend no time in strategic planning because he spent his typical day "putting out fires." I asked him to follow the above process for a month. You can imagine the result. People stopped coming for Frank's answers. They found their own solutions. They worked with their teammates to figure things out. They solved their own problems.

And how did Frank feel? Desolate. He was no longer needed. His experience was no longer called upon. He was miserable. I suggested that he work on that strategic plan he hadn't had time for. His response? "Actually, I don't know how to do a strategic plan."

Many of us go to our comfort level in our everyday work, doing the jobs we know how to do well, even though we have moved to higher level positions. We may not be confident in the role we are in, but we can look confident being the hero for everyone else in the role we used to play. It is time to *create* heroes.

We must make sure that we hold people accountable to their own thinking process and not let them "delegate" up the care and feeding of their monkeys to us.

So let's talk a bit about how we train those we work with to take an assignment and get it done on their own effectively.

How to Get People to "Get it" When You Give an Assignment – Five Easy Steps

Have you ever given a clear assignment and discovered that the final outcome bore no resemblance to what you originally asked for? How does that happen? You are a bright, articulate person. How can your staff get it so wrong so often? Better break out the mirror. You're going to need it.

Who has primary responsibility for effective assignments – the sender or receiver? You probably answered quickly and correctly – it's the sender. Only the sender knows what is in his head and knows if the message is being delivered well. Yet when people come back with the wrong output, we have a tendency to say things like, "Idiots, they never get it right. They didn't listen – again!"

If this is happening to you, chances are that your process for directing your team goes something like this:

You eat, breathe, live and sleep your work. You wake up in the middle of night with a brilliant idea. You swoop into the office the next morning with your Superman cape flying behind you. You gather the troops into a conference room and enthusiastically launch into your idea, starting in the middle of the sentence, middle of the chapter, middle of the book, thinking that they are all right there with you. The problem here is that they haven't been eating, breathing, living and sleeping this stuff exactly like you are. We often finish such enthusiastic presentations with a really profound statement like, "Do you understand? Are there any questions?!"

Of course they say they understand! They don't want to look stupid. And as for questions, they don't know what they don't know. They look like they "get it." They were nodding and smiling, right? That means you have accomplished your goal, shared your message and brilliant idea, and they will go forth and implement with no worries. You can now happily swoop out of the conference room, assuming that having heard your inspirational message. Your team is already at work on getting it done, right? What is really happening in your wake is that the team is asking each other, "What was that?" (Shrugging shoulders and heads shaking all around.)

One of the best definitions I've ever heard for communication is that "it is the art of conveying meaning and obtaining understanding." The piece that's usually missing from effective communication? Obtaining understanding. If you want a simple, five-step plan to ensure that your assignments are heard and that you are obtaining understanding every time, try the power of paraphrase in reverse as outlined here:

1. *Give your assignment as clearly and succinctly as you can, knowing the "end-game" before you start.*

   What is the "bumper sticker" message with which you want to leave them? Make it a practice to verbalize your bumper sticker in your head before you even begin talking.

2. *Once your message is conveyed, test for understanding.*

   Don't ask, "Do you understand?" OR "Make sense?" OR "Any questions?" We should try to eliminate these phrases from our vocabulary. They are rhetorical. Instead, ask the "receiver" to play back or paraphrase the assignment. How close is the play back to your pre-prepared bumper sticker?

But most of us don't take this step because it's uncomfortable – it feels like we're trying to catch them not listening well – OR it feels condescending. For example, "I want to make sure you understand what I just said – play it back for me." It sounds hierarchical and parental. Besides, it all takes time and, heck, we're so darned articulate… why should we waste that time? (Though we have plenty of time to fix the messes that come back later, right?)

Instead, demonstrate that you take full responsibility for message effectiveness as the "sender" of the communication by saying something like, "*I* speak really fast and sometimes leave things out. Can you play back for me what success with this project looks like and why it is so important?" OR "This is really an important assignment and *I* want to make sure *I've* communicated it well. What did you hear?" OR "This next step is really important to your future so *I* want to make sure *I've* explained it well. What did you hear?" Do you see all the *I's* in these statements that put responsibility for effective communication on the sender?

Asking this question while taking the full burden of responsibility seems to be one of the hardest things for a person to do. I often test my workshop participants throughout a session to model this approach and they almost always freeze up, offering phrases like, "I want to make sure *you* understand," or "I want to make sure *you've* got it," both of which blame the receiver for not listening well. See the *you's* in these statements? This is an important distinction. You need to take full responsibility to deliver your message using lots of *I's* in the replay question.

With just a little practice you can become proficient at asking the question the right way, with the burden of responsibility on *you*. You'll know you've done it right when your people feel perfectly comfortable spewing their version of your message with all their horrifying inaccuracy, selective listening and information gaps.

3. **If there are gaps between what the person heard and what you intended, start again and fill in those gaps.**

Don't say, "You have it wrong" OR "No, that's not right." You should assume that *you* didn't communicate clearly enough. Don't look exasperated – it is better to sync up before they go out the door than weeks later after blood, sweat and tears have gone into the project. Explain it differently – use different words and examples.

4. *Ask for the replay until you are in sync with the listener.*

"I want to make sure that I have communicated it well this time; what did you hear?"

Note: Have you ever been frustrated when giving a complex assignment that the receiver wasn't taking notes? Do you usually say something professorial like, "Take out a pen!" after which they do exactly as you suggest and begin to doodle on the page?

Worry less about whether they are gathering the information as you would. Ensure that, no matter how they gather the data, they are able to replay what success looks like. That's what really counts.

5. *Build the expectation among your team that you will end all important communications with a request for replay.*

When people learn that they will be expected to "play back" communication, direction and coaching, they pay much greater attention from the beginning. When a communication or message is really important to you, ask *them* to summarize their commitments, actions, agreements, etc., in a follow-up email. Again, don't for the sake of expediency, do it for them! Find out what *they* took away from the session.

Remember that *Peanuts* teacher character with his nothing message? Do you want people to listen intently when you give an assignment or do you want them to hear "wha, wha, wha, wha, wha"? With a consistent request for replay, they will pay close attention and you will be sure that they actually hear your real message!

Now that we can give clear assignments using the power of replay, let's talk about how to *let go* of control.

How To Let Go With Peace of Mind – Eight Simple Ingredients for your Delegation Soup

Delegation soup? See yourself adding the following ingredients that will make you the best darned delegation chef in town… or at least in your office. Here is what delegation pros do:

1. ***Take a risk.*** Don't give a $10-an-hour job to a $100-an-hour person just so you will feel comfortable that it will get done. Don't demoralize the talent on your team. Give the right level of task to the right person that allows them to stretch.

2. ***Provide context.*** That means the *what* and the *why*. Explain specifically what success will look like and why this assignment is important. If you can't describe success in measurable outcomes, your assignment is not clear.

   An example of a clear *what* explanation would be, "If you are wildly successful this project will be 100% complete by December 1st, it will be $0 over budget and your internal customers, when polled randomly, will rank the project at a 4 out of 5 on its ability to serve their needs."

   An example of a clear *why* explanation would be, "If you are successful with this project, our leadership team will be thrilled to see an improvement in productivity, which will decrease cost. If you are not successful, the team could experience further frustration and the need for continued overtime, and our team is already burning out fast. You could make a real difference here!"

   Don't make the mistake of launching into *how*, such as, "First, schedule a meeting with George, Terry and Cher. You might want to use the second floor conference room where you won't have as many interruptions. Ask the participants this list of questions and bring their summarized responses back to me."

   In the above *how* explanation, we haven't told the person to whom we have delegated the project or task what success looks like and *why* it is important. We haven't even told the individual why we are having the meeting. We are not delegating. We are telling *how*.

Why do we so often delegate in this manner? Because we are control freaks! We've done the job 100 times and know *how* we want it done, which is *our* way. But we haven't thought through *what* success looks like. The following outlines what we should tell new vs. veteran employees about the *how* when delegating:

Employee	How	What and Why
A Newbie	100%	100%
A Veteran	0	100%

On which column should we focus most of our time? Ask yourself where you *usually* focus while delegating. Your job has changed!

Why tell newbies 100% of the *what* and *why*? So when they get stuck (and they will), they have a framework for thinking through the next step. Create an environment wherein new recruits see the big picture as well as the short-term task. Help them *find their own way* to the end result when they can, rather than having to come back to you for more direction. When they are successful, it not only creates enormous pride for the new person but it often generates new innovations for your company. The newbie doesn't know what he can't do!

Why tell a veteran zero of the *how*? Let me ask, how do *you* like being told how to do your job? If we want to avoid being labeled a micro-manager, we need to get comfortable with the idea that if the person successfully achieves a clearly articulated *what* and *why*, within the confines of the rules and values of the company, it doesn't matter *how* they do it, and it doesn't matter that they do it differently than we would. (Ouch!)

3. ***Request the replay.*** Encourage feedback and questions. Without looking at the above explanation that describes *how* to ask for that replay, can you frame a request for replay right now that places the full burden of communication responsibility on *you*? If so, you are one of the rare 2% in this world who can do it the first time. If not, re-read paragraph 2 in the above section on *How to Get People to Get It*, remember using the *I* word, and practice! With just three solid attempts, it will be like riding a bike and you'll be a request-for-replay pro.

4. ***Always give a due date.*** All too often, we delegate with passion,

emotion and sense of urgency, but never mention a due date. Why? We don't want the push back. We're afraid that if we verbalize the needed deadline, the recipient of the task will protest, pointing to the million other deadlines on his or her plate, most of which came from us! So we choose to stay silent, hoping they will see our passion and sense of urgency and make it the next item they tackle.

But what do *you* do with assignments that have no due date? You put them on the bottom of the stack – and your task recipients will do the same. They can't determine if we need it in an hour, tomorrow or next week, so they'll fit it in when they have time. We need to get the push back up front. We must let people know when we need something done and why, or accept the pressure of not knowing when the outcome we need will show up on our desks.

5. *Designate one ultimately accountable party.* As discussed previously, give the entire job to one person. For every major initiative in your office, there should be one, ultimately accountable person. You may be thinking, "Wait a minute! Aren't some jobs too big for one person?"

    Some of my clients like to secretly, behind the scenes, give the same project to two or three people, hoping one of them will follow through. People figure that out pretty quickly and *all* stop following through!

    Or sometimes a project is intentionally assigned to two or three people in a meeting. What happens at the next meeting when progress on the project is requested? Yep. Lots of finger pointing.

    Just because one person is ultimately accountable, it doesn't mean that person has to do it all alone. An individual can pull in other peers and deploy other resources. But if there is no one ultimately accountable party, I guarantee that the project will not be completed successfully.

6. *Require progress reports.* Negotiate them *at the time of delegation.* This is a tool for sleeping peacefully at night after delegating an important task. Outline for the person what success looks like. Using our previous example, tell the person, "This project will be 100% complete by December 1st, it will be $0 over budget and your internal customers, when polled randomly, will

rank the project at a 4 out of 5 on its ability to serve their needs." Explain that you would like to receive a progress report every Friday by 3:00 p.m. with only three bullet points:

- % job completion
- % budget used to date
- The person's best estimation of how the internal customers would rank progress so far on the project's ability to serve their needs

Add these progress report due dates to your calendar.

What should you do if the progress reports indicate that the person is following through consistently and that the project is on or ahead of schedule? You're right. They should be celebrated. Plus, this person has earned something more – a little autonomy! Tell the individual that the progress reports are only needed every *other* week and then keep expanding trust as it is earned.

What should you do if the person is consistently late with the progress reports or the project is not going well? Let's start with late reports. If the report is due at 3:00 p.m. and it isn't there at 3:01 p.m., pick up the phone and ask for status. Remember, you teach people how to treat you, and if they believe you aren't really serious about deadlines, they will justify delays. Don't negotiate with yourself, explaining away their failure to deliver on time. Call them on it. Yes, even if one minute late. Set the expectation for your team up front.

If the progress reports indicate that the project is not going well, this person has earned something too – additional oversight. Tell the individual that the progress reports are now required twice a week – once on Wednesday and again on Friday, both at 3:00 p.m. If they should protest that someone else on the team has been allowed more freedom, having to give reports only every other week, explain that he or she too could earn the same autonomy by being on time and ensuring successful project completion.

You don't want to require progress reports on every project and for every person equally. Use judgment about how many updates you need and use this tool only on longer term, more important objectives. Give your "newbies" less room until they earn more freedom. If you want to avoid micromanagement, give your veterans more rope, but don't abdicate! Don't just hope they'll come through, but rather require a progress update at about half way through the project and again a week or two before completion, so you are comfortable that there will be no surprises.

Think of how much time you spend chasing people for updates on "stuff." Save yourself time and improve your sleep by using quick and easy progress reports to get these same people chasing *you* with updates. Wouldn't *that* be a nice switch?

7. *Use Vince Lombardi's tactics.* Vince Lombardi was one of the most beloved and winning coaches of all time. In the late 1950s a reporter stuck a microphone in his face and asked, "Coach, why is it that every major player wants to play for you?"

Lombardi replied, "Oh, it's pretty simple. When we win, they did it; when we lose, I did it." As you read this "the buck stops here" line, you are probably nodding your head in agreement, assuming that this is *your* philosophy as well. But ask yourself what you would do if the CEO of your organization called you into his office and raked you over the coals for a job poorly performed. The first human reaction? "Tim did it, but I'll make sure it doesn't happen again!" The Vince Lombardi method? "I let you down, and it won't happen again." Does this mean you don't hold Tim accountable? Of course not. You just don't throw Tim under the bus to your CEO.

Conversely, what would you do if the CEO of your organization called you into his office and praised you profusely for a job beautifully performed? The first human reaction? "Thank you!" The Vince Lombardi method? "It was all due to my team – they really shined, didn't they?"

These types of conversations usually happen behind closed doors, but your team always figures out how you have handled them. How? The next time the CEO sees Tim he might glare at him in the hallway. Or he might go out of his way to praise the team for a job well done. They will know how you handled it either way.

One more quick note. One of the most empowering things you can do for your team is to orchestrate opportunities for them to receive secondhand praise. Why is it that they so value secondhand praise from the CEO or someone other than you in the organization? Because they'll know you have been talking nicely about them behind their backs, and there is no more genuine form of recognition.

8. *Avoid overprotecting and sabotage.* Some of us are rescuers. We do it with our kids and we do it in the office. We desperately want people to avoid mistakes, feelings of failure or pain. Or we're simply sure that we can do it better. Either way, we jump in before others get a chance to complete a difficult task and we do it for them.

The unkindest cut is doing for people that which they can and should do for themselves!

In my workshops, I often cite the well-known Disney/Pixar movie, *Finding Nemo*, as a perfect example. In case you don't have kids or haven't seen this classic animated film, here is some background...

Finding Nemo is the story of a of a doting father clownfish named Marlin who after losing his wife and all his other children in a terrible barracuda incident becomes highly protective of his only remaining child, Nemo. Do you know what happens when children are smothered by hovering parents? They are not prepared for the world and they rebel, which Nemo does. As a result, Nemo finds himself captured by a human and the story unfolds as Marlin goes on a quest to recover his son.

On this quest, Marlin runs into another father, a turtle named Crush, who has a very different parenting style. While Crush's children are playing together in the ocean, one of his turtle-sons is suddenly swept away by the very powerful Australian current. In this scene Marlin, wanting to save the little turtle, begins to rush to his rescue. Crush stops him with the line, "Whoa, kill the motor, Dude. Let's see how Squirt does flying solo." After a seemingly endless wait watching Marlin worry with bated breath, the little turtle flies out of the current and back to his family, gushing with pride and excitement about his new swimming feat to which his dad, Crush, responds only with praise and celebration.

The clownfish could have saved the little turtle, but what would have been lost? Pride, confidence and a new experience that will serve Squirt well throughout his life. All of this would have been sabotaged. What kind of leader are you? Do you hover and protect like an overprotective parent clownfish or do you let people try and risk occasional failure like the much wiser, more parentally skilled turtle? If you are honest with yourself, you will know immediately.

Are you still unsure about which is your style? Ask yourself after every interchange with your team whether they come away from interactions with you feeling stronger or weaker? If you are to create heroes, you need to build strength and confidence in people, *which they can only achieve by earning it.* Take a risk. Let others take a risk. People need a chance to try and fail. Start easy. Practice at home, especially if you have children.

Review these eight delegation steps to choose one that would make you an even more effective delegator. You will not only *make* more time for yourself, but you will grow your talent.

This chapter focused on how to get the people who work for you to understand, step up, take charge and excel. The biggest decision you have to make is whether it's okay with you if they do. If it is, you can use the checklists in this chapter to delegate flawlessly every time.

Summary and Action Steps:

1. Teach people to solve their own problems.
2. Become skilled and consistent at asking for replay to test the receiver's understanding of the assignment.
3. Choose one of the eight delegation steps above that if mastered would make you a more effective delegator. Practice that step for 30 days before tackling another.
4. Ask people for feedback on how you are doing as a delegator. If you are doing it well, they will notice very quickly. Those who want to shine will love this approach. Those who want to avoid accountability will hate it. Push past resistance.
5. Remind yourself frequently of your goal. Improving delegation skills is a lifelong journey!

Delegation – the Bumper Sticker: Your job has changed. It is no longer to *be* the hero but to be the *creator* of heroes.

11

Secret 10 – How to Get People to Follow You Anywhere

The 10 essential attributes of the most successful leaders

I have asked thousands of workshop attendees what they think the difference is between a leader and a manager. The usual answer is that a leader is a visionary and the manager is more of a "doer," one who executes the leader's vision. People often say that the leader is more strategic and that the manager is more tactical, or something to that effect. And they would be right! Then, I put them through the following exercise:

I ask them to imagine that I have thrown 40 managers and a leader into a dense rainforest along with a pile of knives and machetes. I tell them that survival is at stake and that they must find the fastest way out – ASAP. I promise, this is not a reality TV show, but rather an important lesson on leadership.

What will the managers do, I ask? They will grab up those machetes and start hacking a path through the forest. They want to see the immediate results of their efforts. Some will hack north, because they think it's the fastest way out. Some will hack a path east, because they think it's the fastest way out. Some will hack northeast, because although it feels farther, it appears less dense and they believe they will get out faster. Some decide to hack a *new* path north, because although they feel that the first group is right about their direction, they feel that that group is hacking too slowly. They'll hack a path right next to them and be the first to get out.

Wise use of resources? Of course not. Our human resource is getting tired. Our knives and machetes are getting dull. What are the chances that we'll get all 41 people out alive, safe and together using this approach? Does it happen in your organization that people who should have the same goal are actually hacking in different directions? What should the leader do?

After a little thought, there is almost always someone in the workshop who correctly yells out, "The leader should climb a tree!" Yes! Get above the treetops to visualize the shape of the rainforest and determine the fastest way out.

Well, I explain, the leader of our story finally did climb the tree. Unfortunately, it took him two weeks to do so and in the meantime his four groups of hackers had made a lot of headway. Blood, sweat and tears had gone into all their efforts over the two week period. Also unfortunately, as he looked over the trees, he discovered that the groups going north were hacking parallel to the forest's edge and those hacking east were going away from the closest way out. The fastest way out was clearly a short distance west. So he tried to get them all to come back to their initial starting place so they could all hack west together. Many resisted.

Why would they resist if the distance were obviously shorter going west? Remember, they had been hacking for two weeks! Too much is invested and ego is at stake. Many would rather work harder and faster to prove their direction right, even if it represents large multiples of work! Does this happen in your organization? Are people so invested in their way that they can't change even when all reality says they should? Do you find that they don't want to be confused by the facts? Note this wisdom from Frederich Nietzsche:

> **Many are stubborn in pursuit of the path they have chosen; few in pursuit of the goal.**

The lesson for the leader? Climb the tree fast!

Get everyone going in the same direction. It is literally better to let your team sit at the bottom of the tree and eat pineapple than to have them all hacking off in different directions. Yet sometimes as leaders we look out on all we survey and we say to ourselves, "Everyone is busy. This is good." Not necessarily, and especially not if your people are all going in different directions.

Some leaders have actually told me that their primary job isn't to be climbing trees and determining vision, but rather to be the lead hacker! Think about that one. Why do leaders love being the lead hacker? Oh, the reasons are endless. They climbed the corporate ladder by being great hackers. They know how to hack; they hack better than anyone. They can get out there, roll up their sleeves and show panicky people how proper hacking should be done. They can go to their comfort zone of competence when they aren't really sure how to climb trees or develop vision, but man, they sure know how to hack! However, hacking is no longer their role. Their role is to be a leader of hackers.

I frequently ask the workshop attendees if it is ever okay for a leader to hack? The answer is yes, but never until the direction is clear and everyone is moving in that same direction. One should never hack as an excuse to avoid being strategic and creating a plan.

Is it okay for a leader to be wrong? The leader of our story has determined that west is the right direction. He finally persuades the team to unite in that direction, and even has his resources allocated so that some are hacking, some are clearing debris, some are sleeping to relieve the hackers and some are preparing food. Without this allocation of resources all would be hacking in a narrow area, and arms and legs would go flying!

With this new well-oiled machine, our team quickly and safely reaches the edge of the forest and discovers that west was indeed the fastest way out. Unfortunately, it is a 500-foot cliff, and they have no equipment with which to rappel. The leader has made a pretty big mistake.

Mistakes are inevitable. It's actually quite comforting to know that we all make them. But which approach represents an easier recovery from error? To move the well-oiled machine hacking west to a new southerly direction or to try to round up all four teams who were originally hacking north and east and get them to go south? Of course, it's the former. The lesson for the leader?

A bad plan is better than no plan.

Plan with the snapshot of information you have and get people moving in the same direction. When information changes, you can all be nimble and move as a united team.

As you read this leadership story, were you thinking about which approach you take, especially when under stress? Do you climb a tree or do you hack? Make a decision today to climb a tree… to play your highest and best role. Get used to the discomfort of not *doing* until you know where you are *going*.

I guarantee that when your next business grenade hits, everything in you will want to pick up that machete and start hacking. It just feels so good to take action. Instead, stop, breathe and decide to do the **right** rather than the *expedient* thing. Climb the tree. This takes enormous discipline, but it becomes much easier when you have made a conscious, proactive decision to do so. The time spent between when the problem starts and when you start "doing" is uncomfortable. Only the best leaders have the discipline to work through their discomfort to stop, think and be visionary. You can be one of them.

So *how* can you be a visionary and successful leader? I just happen to have a list!

The 10 Essential Attributes of the Most Successful Leaders

Successful leaders tend to share the following 10 characteristics in the workplace and beyond:

1. *Creating clarity* – Leaders must have a very clear vision and specific, measurable goals. As described in the rainforest story, it is important for you and the team to know where you are going. The planning bumper sticker says, "If you don't know where you're going, any road you take will get you there." You don't want to be surprised about where you end up, right? If you feel you aren't strategic and don't think you're good at that "vision thing," don't despair. Being visionary isn't something that's baked into one's DNA. You can learn to be strategic. Follow the simple steps in Chapter 3 on business planning and without much effort, you will have a masterful plan.

    And please don't feel that *you* have to know all the answers. In fact, it's better if you don't! I can't tell you how many leaders have engaged me to facilitate their strategic planning session and then worked like demons *before* the session to craft the entire plan themselves. They felt that as leaders if they didn't have the answers that they would be perceived by their teams as weak and that they lack vision.

I ask the attendees of such sessions, including their leaders, to make no preparations, except for a competitive analysis. In addition to that external study, I ask them to bring their latest financials and their brains. That's it. Plans derived from team collaboration and debate are always better than what any one person creates. So use the team. In doing so, you build team ownership of, pride in and enthusiasm for the plan. This makes it much more likely to happen.

Then translate that plan to overall organization and individual team success metrics or goals. Inspect what you expect. Have a system of accountability that ensures effective execution.

2. *Creating heroes* – As we just discussed, you are no longer the hero who solves every problem, fills every gap and has all the great ideas. That's what you did to get yourself promoted to leadership. Now you are a leader of doers. Your job is to create heroes. It requires a whole different skill set. What brought you to this point won't get you where you need to be. You need to subordinate your ego. Focus on helping others to succeed. Be a great coach.

   Use the seven-step coaching formula from Chapter 5 to coach your players to better team and individual performance. Don't look at coaching and honest confrontation as an obligation, but rather the privilege that it is.

   Surround yourself with talent and then deploy that talent effectively. Leaders who realize that they don't have to be the most intelligent, most experienced, most skilled person on the team win. Those who are insecure fail to hire people around them who are better than they are. Use the steps outlined in Chapter 6 to pack your team with talent. Become an incubator of leaders. Become known as someone to whom the organization can look for people who can advance quickly. You will rise with the tide.

   Honor the chain of command and don't undermine your leaders by doing for them that which they should do for themselves.

   Use the "art of the question" from Chapter 7 to help others discover your ideas so they will own and run with them.

Use the delegation steps outlined in Chapter 10 to grow your team talent and their capabilities. Using the checklists in each of these chapters makes taking new approaches more effortless.

Avoid "having to" do it all yourself. If you can surround yourself with superstars, you won't stay in any position for long – you'll be advanced faster than you dreamed possible. Leaders who don't surround themselves with A-players become doomed to stay in the same position forever, because they will always be needed there to play the role of the best darned hackers in the office.

3. ***Learning to serve*** – Servant leadership is about literally turning the organization chart upside down and, as leader, looking for ways to better serve the people who work for you. Your job is to create an environment that draws out their best efforts. How can you remove obstacles and pave the way for their success?

   In too many organizations, I have found that most of the staff feels they are serving their leader. They perceive their manager as "the client." They live most of their workdays trying to please their boss, meet his or her needs, and make sure he or she is happy. Such a mistake – this kind of internal focus is a trap. This energy should be turned externally toward your real clients. What do we need to do to please *them*, meet *their* needs and make sure *they* are happy?

   Randomly question your frontline staff about who they see as their "client." If their responses frequently name internal leaders and managers, you need to teach your managers to serve.

4. ***Crossing the line*** – This is a concept I wish someone had taught me when I first became a manager. What a mess it could have kept me out of had I known...

   Right out of college, I was fortunate to find a wonderful opportunity to participate in a fast-track leadership development program offered by a large commercial insurance company. The program was designed to give up-and-comers like me the opportunity to manage a new department every six months, so we could learn the business quickly while building our management skills in real-time situations. It was a dream job for a novice leader, or so I thought.

My first assignment was to supervise 12 senior underwriters/raters. It was the responsibility of this group to underwrite and develop quotes for complex commercial property insurance. They were all women, and these women were skilled. None had tenure of less than 15 years. And these women were mean.

As their manager, I was tasked each morning to go to a production meeting and to present my projections regarding how many policies my "team" would rate that day. The next day, I would report on the actual number rated and provide the next day's projection. Bottom line? I was to be a leader who consistently improved my team's productivity.

I had learned from the grapevine that "my team" had over the years earned the politically incorrect but amazingly accurate nickname of the "old cows." They would sit lazily in their "pasture," every once in a while looking over their shoulders at the "boss" to decide if the he or she would do anything to motivate them to action. In the meantime, they read paperbacks and talked with each other about politics, the weather, their kids... Well, you get the idea.

They made it clear that they had no respect for me. They made it clear that I had no experience that would help them in any way. And they were right! They laughed at my angst about the next day's production meeting. My team's production numbers continued to decline and my manager was starting to wonder how I had qualified for this fast-track role.

What did I do? I turned the tables. I worked at being really nice, rather than a taskmaster. I brought in homemade brownies, which they ate in the pasture while reading their paperbacks. I gave them quotas, but I explained that these were the expectations of my manager – I certainly wouldn't hold them to such unreasonable standards. I was on their side! Unfortunately, my new approach flopped badly. The production numbers continued to decline. Oh, how I wish someone had taught me about crossing the line.

Referencing the chart below, the theory goes like this. As a leader, you can choose to be on the left (the manager side). Here you are hierarchical, authoritative, hands-off. You are the clear boss. Or you can choose to be on the right (the team side). Here you are friendly, supportive, hands-on and clearly one of the team. Where is the "right" place to be? When asked this question, most of my workshop attendees agree that the right place to be is at the top of the curve – smack in the middle.

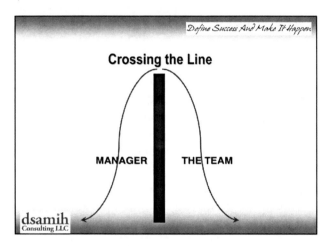

However, they were missing some criteria with which to make this decision, because I failed to inform them that the right place to be is *situational*. Here's how *that* works... If you are a brand new leader, a new boss to the team, like I was with the insurance cows, you start way over on the manager side. You lay down your ground rules and set the tone for how things will be on your watch. There is a new sheriff in town. No matter how effective or ineffective the previous manager was, you will do things differently, and the team needs to understand how you plan to make that work. Outline your expectations that help people understand their boundaries and the rules of the game.

I have a few friends who are elementary school teachers, and they frequently say with a glint in their eyes, "Don't smile until Christmas!" The lesson? You can't begin to be an effective teacher until the class understands that you are its leader. If that isn't clear right from the beginning, those kids can be brutal – they will walk all over a newbie. Yet many novice teachers, like me with the "cows," try to be the nicest, most popular teacher in the school, hoping they can get the kids on their side and then move over to a place of authority.

Mistake! Why do we make this mistake? Because we want to be liked! The lesson?

> ## It is easier to lighten up than to toughen up.

As a new manager, just like a new teacher in grade school, you must set the tone, lay down your ground rules and be sure that you know what they are! The time you invest thinking through your ground rules is time well spent. Otherwise there will be chaos and, like kids, staff will test to see where the boundaries are. Clear and consistent boundaries help people to feel safe. As with the teachers, you can't begin to become an inspirational boss until it is clear that you are the boss.

Only after that can you move up the curve and toward the team. In fact, you must. Why? Because as long as you stay low on the Manager side, people will do what you ask, not because they want to but because they have to. As an inspirational leader, you must capture hearts and minds in order for them to want to deliver *for you*. They must know you genuinely care about them as people. They must know that you will consider their best interests as well as the company's results. They must see you balance hard work with interest in them. Asking about their kids, weekends, stresses, vacations and personal interests does not make you their friend, but rather a concerned and empathetic manager.

You should make time in your day for this kind of authentic discussion. Consider those regularly scheduled MBWAs (Management By Walking Around) that we discussed in Chapter 7 to grow closer to them as people – those of you who already do this know how rewarding it is to truly connect with the people on your team.

But while you can be a concerned manager, be sure to never ever *cross the line*! You are not a member of the team. You don't want to be. You are the team's manager.

Let's be clear on what it means to "cross the line." Leaders who cross the line tell someone on the team something that is confidential or something that criticizes the company, boss or another team player. They cross the line when they explain that an unpopular decision or assignment is their *boss*'s fault (like I did with the cows) rather than supporting and taking full responsibility for that decision themselves. Gossiping with someone on the team about others in the company crosses the line.

Choosing an individual team member as an "insider" sounding board is one of the most insidious of crossing-the-line offenses. Some leaders say to themselves, "But I only tell one person – a mature confidant who wouldn't tell anyone else." Right.

Crossing the line means doing for their teams that which they should do for themselves or protecting them from the outcomes of their actions, buffering them from accountability and making excuses for their mistakes rather than holding them accountable.

Probably the most egregious infraction and most difficult to remedy is being a social "friend" outside of work with someone who reports to them. It just doesn't work.

Why do leaders need to be vigilant? Crossing the line undermines their authority as leaders, because they lose credibility when they are "one of the team." When "the chosen" see the manager as a personal friend, they feel "protected" from adverse leadership decisions, and when they need an important decision to be made they will often go around that leader to his or her manager, the perceived seat of authority.

When *others* see someone on the team as the boss's personal friend, they also believe that person is protected and that they are getting inside "scoop." This creates the perception of both insiders and outsiders, which creates politics and factions on the team. Make no mistake; even if there is only one inside confidant, everyone on the team knows who the insiders and outsiders are.

Because people love to be insiders, they will often ask or encourage their managers to do things that cross the line. And it is tempting to do so, because you will be liked and you can feel a sense of camaraderie and validation. It is lonely at the top! You *do* need someone to talk to, but choose a peer or mentor for that role – not one of the team. Your team members have plenty of friends. What they need in you is a consistent leader who builds a winning team.

I can feel it across the page that you may recognize yourself in this story and are feeling some guilt here. What should you do if you have drifted over the line, which most of us have at one time or another? What should you do if you've been *promoted* from the team to the Manager side? That's even more difficult, because just yesterday, you were gossiping, rolling eyes and criticizing the boss with your team members and now you must be their manager!

As you've probably guessed, in both cases, you must now go way over to the low Manager side. But in both these situations, you must take one preliminary step. If you have drifted over the line, don't just begin being distant and authoritative – people will think you are angry with them or are just in a bad mood. You must have the courage to talk with your team, acknowledge your mistake, and let them know exactly what you've done in the past that you now plan to change. Tell them, "I'm afraid I've been gossiping or talking negatively about the company, or blaming the boss, etc. I realize that this is not the behavior of an excellent leader. I plan to change it immediately. Here is what you can expect to see from me going forward." Tell them what you plan to do differently and why. Remind them, "You don't need another friend – you need a strong leader who will work with each of you fairly to build a successful team."

If you have just been promoted, don't go directly to the Manager side or people will feel that your promotion has gone to your head. Similarly, talk with the team. Let them know how your behavior will change as their leader and why you must change it.

If this crossing-the-line concept resonates with you, make a conscious decision to change your leadership situation and create a plan to make it happen. Don't wing it. If you are consistent, you will witness an enormous difference in your leadership authority and in your team's results. Not so difficult, right?

5. *Demanding Excellence* – Executives often ask if I think it's okay to have such high expectations of the team. Could it be that they are pushing too hard or expecting too much? Are they burning out their teams?

High expectations are a must as long as priorities are clear, reasonable and well communicated. Think back on your career and at an accomplishment that stands out for you. Really, take a few minutes. What jumps out as a major feat of which you are truly proud?

I have asked over 200 high level leaders about the proudest moment in their careers. I almost always hear some version of the answer I received from Rick, a highly successful real estate developer and investor who said with a hint of emotional nostalgia. He said, "I was working with a really great team and we achieved something that most people thought was impossible."

Wouldn't Steve Jobs with his iPhone, iPod and iPad have said the same? How about Jeff Bezos with Amazon and Kindle, and Tony Hsieh with Zappos? How many people would have believed 10 years ago they couldn't be without their treasured iDevice, their e-book or their high-end shoes delivered for free the next day?

Let your team know that you are collectively going to achieve something amazing and that you are expecting them to play their part. Let them know what success looks like and how they can best contribute. Give them the opportunity everyone wants to make a real difference somewhere.

When you find dissention on the team, people not getting along and focusing on petty arguments, you can be sure they are not focused on a large enough mutual goal. Raise the bar! It seems counterintuitive, but when teams aren't working well, raise the stakes. Sports history is packed with stories of down-and-out teams that lacked cohesiveness, talent and teamwork who, even before they found a way to win consistently, set their sights on the state championship. Movies based on true stories like *Hoosiers* and *Remember the Titans* are about teams who were led by coaches who thought big, decided to do something amazing, and then demanded and received excellence from their teams.

Go all out – put it all on the field. Excellence is the only thing that excites passion. When *you* have it your team will too.

6. *Keeping it true* – You can go wrong with most of these leadership qualities and still recover as long as you honestly address your mistakes with your team. An integrity breach, unfortunately, doesn't usually work

that way. Once you've made the integrity error it is much more difficult to recover. People like following leaders who are consistent and dependable in "doing the right thing when no one is looking." This great quality engenders the kind of trust that allows people to tolerate and support unpopular decisions, heavy workloads and tough deadlines, because they believe that they are happening for the right reasons.

Another important aspect of keeping it true is to be absolutely 100% predictable. People need to know where you stand, what you will tolerate and what you won't. This gives them comfort that they can predict their futures and feel safe.

When leaders fail to do what they say they are going to do, when their behavior is inconsistent, when they grab credit or cut corners on values, they send the message that they are slippery, manipulative and not to be trusted. No one follows such a leader without one eye over their shoulder looking for the trap this person is likely to set for them. No way, in such an environment, will these leaders receive the full energy and commitment of their team.

Set the standard. Be a positive role model your team can count on and emulate. You will be rewarded with trust and loyalty.

7. *Keeping it light* – After an especially intense but rewarding leadership workshop, one of the participants named Mitch stayed to speak with me after the other attendees had left. Mitch explained that it was clearer to him than ever before, based on the 360 results delivered in the workshop, that he needed to work on this "sense of humor thing." Just the way he said it scared me a little, but we talked about the importance of diffusing tension and lightening the workload in the office with humor.

He worried that he would have to learn to tell jokes and to master joke timing and delivery. On the contrary, I explained. Jokes often come off badly and are often not received as intended. Many are off-color and offensive, and you are frequently safer in the work environment without them.

Reassured, he went back to his office, committed to building a sense of humor. Unfortunately, he worried that the self-effacing humor we had discussed using in the workshop would make him appear "too vulnerable to the troops." The funny thing is that this guy wasn't even in the military. Anyway, he called a few months later to confide in me that "this sense of humor thing has backfired." I asked him what had gone wrong.

He explained, "I decided to have a quick all-hands meeting once a month to communicate more effectively with the troops and to demonstrate my new sense of humor."

Uh, oh! I saw it coming.

He continued, "So I would pick someone out from the crowd and make fun of them in a humorous way."

Danger, danger!! Not even Don Rickles was able to pull this off consistently without hurting feelings and creating enemies.

Real leaders don't get a laugh at someone else's expense. They need to get comfortable enough with themselves and their teams to be vulnerable and poke fun at themselves. People love working for people who don't take themselves too seriously and who initiate laughter at their own expense.

Mitch's problem was what I call the beach ball syndrome. Have you ever tried to hold a beach ball under water for any length of time? It takes enormous strength and energy, and unless you are doing it for exercise it is a colossal waste of time.

Leaders who try to pretend that they are perfect and that they have all the answers put this beach ball kind of energy into "appearing" perfect. From the minute they leave the house in the morning they try to hide their defects, insecurities and weaknesses. In doing so they loudly *broadcast* their insecurity! Heck, people know they're not perfect and they talk about their leaders' foibles in the coffee room anyway. Such leaders should let that beach ball come up for air and out of the water. They can then use that energy to lead their teams rather than to try to disguise the un-disguisable. Then their people will laugh with them instead of *at* them.

Most of our jobs don't involve life-or-death situations. Leaders should take themselves less seriously. Practice self-deprecating humor at home. Your family will love you for it, and you'll feel more comfortable trying it at work.

8. *The know-it-all trap* – Have you ever worked for a know-it-all? What's the first thing you wanted to see happen to that person? You wanted them to fail, right? Well, the quickest road to a leader's failure is to surround him or herself with people who *want* to see them fail. They will make it happen! Leaders should be humble and celebrate ideas and decisions that don't come from them. Note this bit of wisdom from champion UCLA basketball coach, John Wooden:

> **Talent is God-given; be humble. Fame is man-given; be thankful. Conceit is self-given; be careful.**

9. *Being brave* – Great leaders must appear confident. Imagine that leader in the rainforest, coming down out of the tree and addressing his exhausted troops who had been hacking in multiple directions for weeks and saying something like, "Guys, I think west is the right way to go. I'm not sure. I can't tell if this is right. We're probably all going to die anyway, so let's give it a go!" His troops would quickly go back to their original paths and start hacking again in their own various directions.

Confidence is much easier to muster when you know a deep dark secret that I learned from the wonderful leaders with whom I've been privileged to work over the years, a secret I will share with you now...

In 2009, in an attempt to understand the impact of the economic crash on my clients' and their companies' futures, I interviewed 250 senior executives and asked them just one question: What is the one thing that most keeps you up at night? The most frequent response by far did not involve the economy, global competition or what our government was doing to address it all. The most frequent answer went something like this, "I fear that someone is going to find me out. They'll discover I'm not qualified to be here as their leader."

People are fragile. Leaders are fragile. They have doubts. For most executives, no one is more critical of them than themselves. When you know that everyone else has doubts, too, it's easier to be brave. Take a risk. Chart a course. Engage the team. Go for it. Remember that a bad plan is better than no plan, so change course when you receive new information, but give people confidence that you know what you're doing. And when you just don't feel it? Fake it 'til you make it! Okay, one more story...

As president of a health care company, I made it a practice to do a MBWA each morning at the office. One day, after learning of one of a loved one's passing, I walked in sadly, went straight to my office and went to work, skipping the usual MBWA. I was shocked later that day to find that several frontline employees, worried about my moodiness, came into the office to ask if they were soon to be laid off.

You see, they are not really worried about your demeanor; they are worried about what your disposition means for them. Don't kid yourself. Your people watch your every move and mannerism. They look for the early clue that something is wrong and that their jobs and futures might be affected. If you present a calm, confident demeanor, you create an environment that allows them to feel safe.

And, remember, that to which you pay the most attention happens. If you pay attention to politics, gossip and future speculations about the organization then that is what your team will pay most attention to. If you pay most attention to measurable results, performance and customer satisfaction, that is what your team will focus on, too. Decide to focus confidently on what most matters. Your team will do the same and you will be an even more successful leader.

When leaders project insecurity, their people will not only know it, but they will feel uncomfortable, slow their productivity and perhaps even start hacking in a different direction. When leaders project confidence, people will feel it and follow them anywhere.

10. ***Being cool*** – Style is probably the most amorphous of all the leadership attributes. It's one of those qualities that you simply recognize when you see it. Think about leaders who have style. I often ask workshop attendees to identify leaders who *they* think have style and they frequently mention people like John F. Kennedy, Ronald Reagan, Bill Clinton, Colin Powell, Oprah Winfrey, Mother Theresa and Nelson Mandela. I then ask them to identify what it is that these leaders have in common. Is it their politics, their intelligence, their communication technique, their humor? No, they respond, it isn't exactly any of these qualities. Then what *is* it?

The simple secret shared by these famous leaders is that they were each comfortable in his/her own skin. But even more than that it is to be unique, to have a different little quirk, and rather than hiding that quirk to conform to others they embrace their uniqueness and even flaunt it! They exude confidence in their differences and encourage others to do the same. Nelson Mandela once famously said:

> **It is our light, not our darkness that most frightens us. There's nothing enlightened about shrinking so that other people won't feel insecure around you. We were born to make manifest the glory of God that is within us. It's not just in some of us; it's in everyone. And as we let our own light shine, we unconsciously give other people permission to do the same.**

People love following leaders with style. Let's face it, Bill Clinton messed up on several of the 10 essential leadership qualities listed above, but *style* got him through it and he continued to be an influential leader. Add to your considerable qualities a little style, a little savoir faire, a little "I don't care what others think, this is right and I'm going to fight for it" style. See what happens. You might be surprised how quickly others respond. And if you worry so much about what others think that you are afraid to put it out there and create your own style, remember the wisdom of Mark Twain:

> **You would worry less about what others thought about you if you realized how seldom they do.**

Every one of the leadership attributes we've discussed in this chapter can be learned and improved upon. No one is born with all these qualities. And although you are probably already demonstrating many of these attributes, the truly exceptional leaders are constantly looking for ways to grow their skills, which is in fact why you are reading this book. If you want to enhance your talent, focus on just one of these ten attributes that would take your leadership skill up yet another notch.

Summary and Action Steps:

1. Choose just one of the essential leadership concepts in this chapter that

you believe most important to taking your leadership skills to a new level, such as creating heroes, learning to serve or crossing the line.

2. Highlight that section and practice the steps for correcting that one issue.

3. Practice at home with family and friends – and definitely at work – until you have turned that particular attribute into a leadership strength. Taking these sections one at a time is much easier, because it will hold top-of-mind awareness for you.

4. Tell people the skill you are working to improve and ask them for their honest feedback on how you are doing. You will see *your* number of followers grow!

Leadership – the Bumper Sticker: A leader is someone who has followers.

12

Putting It All Together
What can you do NOW?

It sometimes happens after attending one of my leadership workshops that participants get pretty fired up. They tend to go back to the office, gather their teams and say something enthusiastic like, "We're going to establish goals, inspect what we expect, climb a tree and eat the frog!" Please don't do this after reading my book.

Your employees will think that little green aliens kidnapped you, abused you on their home planet and dropped you back to earth. Don't overwhelm them with jargon, enthusiasm or cult-like behavior. We'll be guilty of becoming the flavor of the month I talked about in the first chapter.

You have an opportunity to take just a few nuts and bolts concepts that we've reviewed here and make a lasting change that can positively impact your team and your career.

Remember that at the beginning of the book your assignment was to find only two or three ideas that would help you take your team to the next level of performance. Take a moment now to decide which concepts from this book resonated most for you, which in the workshop we would call your most important DSAMIH moments.

The following bumper sticker reminders from each chapter might help jog your memory:

Chapter 1:   Define success and make it happen!

Chapter 2:   Cascade goals throughout your organization and inspect what you expect!

Chapter 3:   If you don't know where you're going, any road will get you there.

Chapter 4:   You master your life when the voice of your inner vision is louder than all other voices.

Chapter 5:   Leaders have the courage to repair or replace!

Chapter 6   Create an environment that is a magnet for talent – it will be your greatest competitive advantage.

Chapter 7:   The single biggest problem in communication is the illusion that it has taken place.

Chapter 8:   Leadership is about unlocking the potential of the fine and unselfish person everyone believes themselves to be.

Chapter 9:   You have the power to manage time; it doesn't have to manage you!

Chapter 10:   Your job has changed. It is no longer to be the hero but to be the creator of heroes.

Chapter 11:   A leader is someone who has followers.

Go back to your highlights and narrow them down to those that most grabbed you as relevant to your situation. Make a conscious decision to practice the two or three techniques you have selected until they feel like habits. If you focus on them for 20 to 30 days, they will come easily to you going forward. Once these are mastered, choose a couple more. Take it slowly, implement carefully and involve your team in the process. It's not that difficult, and it will reap big rewards.

You can make a longer list of lessons if you like and put them in priority order, but choosing only two or three to implement initially is essential. You can keep top-of-mind change in three major areas, but it is difficult to make more than three fundamental changes at once. Focus on the important few... *for you and your team*. Leaders who try to adopt many changes simultaneously always face the inevitable daily business grenades, and they revert to old behaviors. Make the time you invested reading this book work for you over the long term.

I cherish the lessons that I have learned over the years from the amazing clients I have been privileged to serve and which I have shared here with you. It is my sincere hope that after reading this book you can say you have learned at least two important lessons that you won't soon forget and which, when implemented, will launch you to a new level of leadership success.

Armed with these lessons, and as you decide how you can best *Define Success And Make It Happen*, I challenge you with the poem from Linda Ellis that I share at the end of each DSAMIH leadership workshop:

The Dash

I once knew a reverend
who spoke at the funeral of his friend.
He referred to the dates on her tombstone
from the beginning to the end.

He noted first the date of her birth
and spoke of the following date with tears,
But he said what mattered most of all
was the dash between those years.

For that dash represented
all the time she'd spent on earth.
Now only those who loved her
knew what that little line was worth.

It matters not how much we own
the cars... the house... the cash.
What matters is how we live and love
and how we spend our dash.

So think about it long and hard...
Are there things you'd like to change?
You know not how much time is left;
are you at dash "mid-range?"

Vicki Merrill conducts keynote speeches and workshops on the following topics in addition to many customized programs:

- Strategic Planning
- Executive Coaching
- Personal Life Planning
- Conflict Management
- Team Building
- Packing Your Team with A-Players
- The Leadership Edge
- Moments of Truth Customer Service
- Time Management

Please contact her for more information at: www.dsamih.com.

If you implement lessons from this book, Vicki would be eager to hear your stories and how they worked for you! Please send her an email through her site.

Lightning Source UK Ltd.
Milton Keynes UK
UKOW05f0025130214

226376UK00015B/457/P